TRAVERSE
THEATRE

Traverse Theatre Company
The Juju Girl
by Aileen Ritchie

cast in order of appearance

Kate/Catherine	Susan Vidler
Andrew/Ozzie	Derek Riddell
Daniel	Manu Kurewa
Eddie	Kolade Agboke
Precious/Jayne	Ulla Mahaka
Martha	Eyahra Mathazia
Joshua	Tumaini Lambo

other parts played by members of the Company

director	John Tiffany
designer	Laura Hopkins
choreographer	De-Napoli Clarke
composer	John Irvine
lighting designer	Conleth White
stage manager	Victoria Paulo
deputy stage manager	Chloë Ribbens
assistant stage manager	Mike Fitton
wardrobe supervisor	Lynn Ferguson
wardrobe assistants	Caitlin Blair
	Carolyn Davies

**First performed at the Traverse Theatre
Friday 6 August 1999**

KT-170-770

TRAVERSE THEATRE

One of the most important theatres in Britain The Observer

Edinburgh's **Traverse Theatre** is Scotland's new writing theatre, with a 36 year record of excellence. With quality, award-winning productions and programming, the Traverse receives accolades at home and abroad from audiences and critics alike.

The Traverse has an unrivalled reputation for producing contemporary theatre of the highest quality, invention and energy, commissioning and supporting writers from Scotland and around the world and facilitating numerous script development workshops, rehearsed readings and public writing workshops. The Traverse aims to produce several major new theatre productions plus a Scottish touring production each year. It is unique in Scotland in its exclusive dedication to new writing, providing the infrastructure, professional support and expertise to ensure the development of a sustainable and relevant theatre culture for Scotland and the UK.

Traverse Theatre Company productions have been seen worldwide including London, Toronto, Budapest and New York. Recent touring successes in Scotland include PERFECT DAYS by Liz Lochhead (January - March '99), PASSING PLACES by Stephen Greenhorn, HERITAGE by Nicola McCartney and LAZYBED by Iain Crichton Smith. PERFECT DAYS is currently playing at the Vaudeville Theatre in London's West End.

The Traverse can be relied upon to produce more good-quality new plays than any other Fringe venue
Daily Telegraph

During the Edinburgh Festival the Traverse is one of the most important venues with world class premieres playing daily in the two theatre spaces. The Traverse won *ten* awards at the 1998 Edinburgh Festival Fringe, including *Scotsman Fringe Firsts* for Traverse productions KILL THE OLD TORTURE THEIR YOUNG by David Harrower and PERFECT DAYS by Liz Lochhead.

An essential element of the Traverse Company's activities takes place within the educational sector, concentrating on the process of playwriting for young people. The Traverse flagship education project BANK OF SCOTLAND CLASS ACT offers young people in schools the opportunity to work with theatre professionals and see their work performed on the Traverse stage. In addition the Traverse Young Writers group, led by professional playwrights, has been running for over three years and meets weekly.

AILEEN RITCHIE

Aileen Ritchie was co-founder of Clyde Unity Theatre before going to the National Film and Television School. Since graduating from the screenwriters' course in 1996 she has written and directed *Double Nougat* for BBC Scotland and has just directed her first feature film for Fox Searchlight. *The Juju Girl* is her first full length commission for the Traverse, marking both her return to theatre and her return to Scotland.

FOREWORD

My first plane ticket to Zimbabwe was the single most expensive purchase I had ever made. It was the trip of a lifetime. I believed I was going to travel a strange new continent where everything would be different. I was wrong.

Travelling in from Harare airport in the back of an open truck, I noticed a road sign - Kirkintilloch Avenue. Then an African bus - destination Glenview. My first walk down First Street took me to the Woolworths of my childhood. They even had Pick 'n' Mix sweets. In Bulawayo, McLeish the butcher sold fresh haggis. The only other guest in the hotel lounge was devotedly reading the People's Friend.

I went to discover Africa and found a different kind of Scotland. It made me think a lot about my own identity and history. It was the first time I had felt embarrassed about being Scottish. It was a difficult and strange experience but one which inspired the idea of this play.

Having the idea was the easy bit.

It has taken me a long time to put pen to paper on this and I have a number of people to thank for helping me along the way. My friends and family in Zimbabwe who were patient, helpful and supportive in getting me over my culture shock. My Scottish friends and family who have been my travelling companions on more recent trips and who have shared mosquito repellent, long train journeys and the experience of seeing the Victoria falls.

The Traverse Theatre staff have been endlessly encouraging. From early association with Ian Brown and Ben Twist, then in showing the first samples of script to Ella Wildridge and John Tiffany. They have succeeded in getting a great cast and crew together to collaborate with.

BIOGRAPHIES

Kolade Agboke *(Eddie)*: Trained: Guildhall School of Music and Drama. For the Traverse: WINDOWS ON THE WORLD: NIGERIA AND ZIMBABWE. Other theatre work includes: AN ENCHANTED LAND (Riverside); FOOD FOR THOUGHT (Soho); THE MERCHANT OF VENICE (Sheffield Crucible). Television work includes: THE BILL (guest lead playing Dean Young); MAISIE RAINE (Fair Game Films); THE LONGEST MEMORY (Channel 4).

De-Napoli Clarke (movement director): Trained: The Northern School of Contemporary Dance, Leeds. His work has taken him across Europe and throughout many educational institutions. He joined RJC Dance Company, Leeds, in 1993 and has performed in, and choreographed pieces for Our Hearts Cry Out, Shared Testament, Captured Passionelle, Language, Life, Respect and Jus'Eazy. Theatre work includes work with West Yorkshire Playhouse.

Laura Hopkins (designer): Designs include: KES, DEALER'S CHOICE (West Yorkshire Playhouse); LA TRAVIATA (Castleward Opera); ROBERTO ZUCCO (RSC); FALSTAFF (Opera North, ENO); CANDIDE, LEONCE AND LENA (Gate); BAILAIGANGAIRE (Royal Court); LOOK BACK IN ANGER, CRIMES OF THE HEART (Royal Exchange); RAKE'S PROGRESS (WNO); CARNIVALI, PEEP SHOW, BLOOD, IF WE HAD SHADOWS, A PLAGUE ON BOTH YOUR HOUSES, CLAIR DE LUZ (all in collaboration with director Pete Brooks for Benchtours Theatre Company and Insomnia Productions.

John Irvine (composer): THE JUJU GIRL is John's 15th production for the Traverse. Other theatre includes: BEGIN AGAIN, QUIET NIGHT IN (KtC); TRAINSPOTTING (Traverse/Citizens'/Bush); LAVOCHKIN 5, SEA URCHINS (Tron); WHITE BIRD PASSES (Dundee Rep); PETER PAN (TAG); JEKYLL AND HYDE (Royal Lyceum).

Manu Kurewa *(Daniel)*: For the Traverse: WINDOWS ON THE WORLD: NIGERIA AND ZIMBABWE. Other theatre work includes community touring. Before arriving in Scotland Manu worked with youth groups in Bulawayo, Zimbabwe, devising plays that voiced community concerns. Manu has spent the last three years studying at the National Film and Television School.

Tumaini Lambo *(Joshua)*: Trained: Bagamoyo College of Performing Arts. His acting, dance and teaching has taken him across Europe as well as his native Tanzania. Recent performances include: THE TEMPEST (International Drama Festival) and at the new Earth Centre in Doncaster. He is Artistic Director and Choreographer of the Bugaboo Dance Company.

Ulla Mahaka *(Precious/Jayne)*: Trained: UNESCO Film and TV School. Theatre work includes: SAXONS AND GAULS, GOLDEN MASK OF AGAMEMNON, THE FACTORY CHILDREN, HIAWATHA, TEA FOR TWO. TV work includes: AFRICAN JOURNEY (Jordan/Canada); TSITSI (Sweden); SOLDIER SOLDIER (Carlton UK). Film includes: FLAME (Black and White, Zimbabwe), and MASTERS OF THE ELEPHANTS (City 2000, France). Ulla also works as an Assistant Director, Production Assistant/Coordinator, models part time and is a freelance journalist. She is one of ten African students selected as part of the African Script Development Fund to produce an original screenplay, and is associated with the UNESCO Film and Video Project for Southern Africa.

Eyahra Mathazia *(Martha)*: Theatre work includes: Assistant Director of Os Baianos Theatre Dance Company; A GIRL NAMED HANNAH (Zimbabwe/Mozambique); POSITIVE (Zimbabwe); TAKADINI MT STORY (South Africa); SHOO-GAH (Zimbabwe); FAUST (Zimbabwe/Germany); IVHU VERSUS THE STATE (Zimbabwe); FOX AND THE HOUND (South Africa); CITIZEN CHI (Zimbabwe/Edinburgh). Musicals include: JOSEPH AND HIS TECHNICOLOUR DREAMCOAT (Zimbabwe, winning the ATS Best Actress Award, 1994); MO'TOWN (Zimbabwe). Films include: THE BIG TIME (Zimbabwe); THINKING ABOUT AFRICA (Italy); FOUNTAIN FOR SUSAN (Slovakia); CONGO (Zimbabwe); LUMUMBA: THE RETURN TO CONGO (France); SHADES OF THE CITY (Zimbabwe); TIDES OF GOLD (Zimbabwe/South Africa, award winning documentary at the Cannes Film Festival, 1998). Eyarha also works as a singer and model.

Derek Riddell *(Andrew/Ozzie)*: Trained: L.A.M.D.A. Theatre work includes: ANNA KARENINA (Shared Experience); TRUE WEST (Salisbury & Plymouth); MUCH ADO ABOUT NOTHING (Royal Exchange); THE GLASS MENAGERIE, THE DAUGHTER-IN-LAW (Clwyd); THE BIG PICNIC (Glasgow); MEASURE FOR MEASURE, DON JUAN (Oxford Stage). Television and film work includes: CORONATION STREET (Granada); THE BILL (Thames); CASUALTY, FOR VALOUR: JOHN CRUIKSHANK STORY; STRATHBLAIR (BBC); STRIKE FORCE (Yorkshire); TAGGART (STV). Film work includes: TO HELL WITH LOVE, BROKEN HEART.

John Tiffany (director): Trained: Glasgow University. John has been Literary Director for the Traverse since 1997 where he has directed DANNY 306 + ME (4 EVER) (also Birmingham Rep and tour), PERFECT DAYS (also Citizens', Hampstead, Vaudeville and tour), GRETA, PASSING PLACES (97 & 98) and SHARP SHORTS and co-directed STONES AND ASHES. Other theatre includes: HIDE AND SEEK and BABY, EAT UP (LookOut); THE SUNSET SHIP (Young Vic); GRIMM TALES (Leicester Haymarket); EARTHQUAKE WEATHER (Starving Artists). Film includes: KARMIC MOTHERS (BBC Tartan Shorts) and GOLDEN WEDDING (BBC Two Lives).

Susan Vidler *(Kate/Catherine)*: Trained: Welsh College of Music and Drama. Theatre work includes SABINA (Bush), TRAINSPOTTING (Traverse/Citizens'/Bush); THE PRESENT (Bush/Royal Court); HEARTLESS (ICA); A BETTER DAY (Stratford); THE EMPERORS NEW CLOTHES (Man Act). Television includes: SEX IN THE TWENTY FIRST CENTURY (Red Productions); THE JUMP (Warner Sisters); KAVANAGH QC (Carlton); THE WOMAN IN WHITE, MACBETH ON THE ESTATE, STONE COLD, FLOWERS OF THE FOREST, CASUALTY, DARK ADAPTED EYE (BBC); CRACKER (Granada). Film includes: THE WEDDING TACKLE (Viking); TRAINSPOTTING (Figment/C4); NAKED (Thin Man). Short films include: INSOMNIA (Blue Orange); CALIFORNIA SUNSHINE (Sigma/C4); MEMORY MAN (RDF TV); CLUELESS (Curious).

Conleth White (lighting designer): Recent lighting design includes: NORTHERN STAR (Field Day/Tinderbox, Belfast Festival); BINLIDS (Dubblejoint/Justus, West Belfast, New York); LA TRAVIATA (Castleword Opera); FASHION SHOW (Glasgow School of Art); THE SKY CHAIR (Project Centre, Dublin). Conleth has also designed lighting for Amharclann de Hide, Andrew's Lane, Aisling Ghéar, Calypso, Dock Ward, Druid, Everyman Palace, Firkin Crane, Gaiety, Galloglass, Gate, Glasshouse, Groundwork, Island, Lyric, Passion Machine, Pigsback, Playwrights and Actors, Point Fields, Punchbag, Red Kettle, Rough Magic, Second Age, Smock Alley, Story Tellers, and Wet Paint.

Sets, props and costumes for *The Juju Girl*
created by Traverse Workshops
(funded by the National Lottery)

Kevin Low *production photography*
Euan Myles *print photography*

For generous help on *The Juju Girl*
the Traverse thanks:

the actors who workshopped the play
Ajay Chhabr . Andrew Whaley
The British Council, Zimbabwe and London
Royal Lyceum Theatre . BLF . STV

LEVER BROTHERS for wardrobe care

SPONSORSHIP

Sponsorship income enables the Traverse to commission and produce new plays and offer audiences a diverse and exciting programme of events throughout the year.

We would like to thank the following companies for their support throughout the year.

✕ BANK OF SCOTLAND

CORPORATE ASSOCIATE SCHEME

LEVEL ONE
Balfour Beatty
Scottish Life the PENSION company
United Distillers & Vintners

LEVEL TWO
NB Information
Laurence Smith - Wine Merchants
Willis Corroon Scotland Ltd
Wired Nomad

LEVEL THREE
Alistir Tait FGA
Antiques & Fine Jewellery
Allingham & Co, Solicitors
KPMG
McCabe Partnership
Chartered Accountants
Nicholas Groves Raines
Architects
Scottish Post Office Board

with thanks to
Navy Blue Design, print designers for the Traverse
and to George Stewarts the printers.
Purchase of the Traverse Box Office and computer network has been made possible with funds from the National Lottery.

the Traverse Theatre's work would not be possible without the support of

THE SCOTTISH ARTS COUNCIL ·EDINBVRGH·
THE CITY OF EDINBURGH COUNCIL

the Traverse receives financial assistance for its educational and development work from

John Lewis Partnership, Binks Trust, Peggy Ramsay Foundation, The Yapp Charitable Trusts, The Bulldog Prinsep Theatrical Fund, Calouste Gulbenkian Foundation. The Traverse has the support of The Mackintosh Foundation under the Regional Theatre Young Director Scheme administrated by Channel Four Television. The Theatre has the support of the Pearson Playwrights' Scheme sponsored by Pearson plc.
The Traverse infra-red system is funded by the ADAPT Trust.
Traverse Theatre Charity No. SC002368

TRAVERSE THEATRE - THE COMPANY

Jeremy Adderley
Bar Café Manager

Maria Bechaalani
Deputy Electrician

Caitlin Blair
Wardrobe Assistant

Carolyn Davis
Wardrobe Assistant

Janet Dick
Cleaner

John Dyer
Head Chef

Lynn Ferguson
Wardrobe Supervisor

Jean Fitzsimons
Box Office Manager

David Freeburn
Assistant Box Office Mgr

Michael Fraser
Theatre Manager

Gary Glen
Café Supervisor

Mike Griffiths
Production Manager

Jayne Gross
Acting Development Mgr

David Harrower
Resident Playwright

Zinnie Harris
Associate Playwright

Noelle Henderson
Development Manager

Jamie Higgins
2nd Chef

Philip Howard
Artistic Director

Louise Ironside
Associate Playwright

Lorna Irvine
Class Act Co-ordinator

Miriam Lea
Marketing & Press Asst

Mark Leese
Design Associate

Yvonne McDevitt
RTYDS Assistant Director

Catherine MacNeil
Assistant Administrator

Jan McTaggart
Marketing & Press Officer

Lucy Mason
Administrative Producer

Lorraine May
Front of House Manager

David Moore
Finance & Personnel Mgr

Brian Mundie
Marketing & Press Asst

Duncan Nicoll
Deputy Bar Manager

Pauleen Rafferty
Finance & Personnel Asst

Catherine Robertson
Administrative Assistant

Renny Robertson
Chief Electrician

Angelo Rodrigues
Kitchen Assistant

Hannah Rye
Literary Assistant

Richard Stembridge
Production Assistant

Fiona Sturgeon
Marketing Manager

John Tiffany
Literary Director

Chris Traquair
Stage Technician

Kris Whitehead
Carpenter

ALSO WORKING FOR THE TRAVERSE

Louise Anderson, Paul Axford, Nancy Birch, Sarah Louise Bowman, Alex Chapman, Anna Copland, Andrew Coyle, Rob Evans, Ben Ewart-Dean, Jackie Franklin, Hilary Galloway, Linda Gunn, David Henderson, David Inverarity, Louise Kemp, Judith Keston, Linda Keys, Natasha Lee-Walsh, Sophie Logan, Eilidh Macdonald, Iona Macdonald, Graeme Maley, Nadia Mejjati-Alami, Nadine Mery, Iain Morrison, Simon Muller, Rowan Paton-Risby, Sarah Shiel, Ben Thomson, Lucy Walsh, Josie Ward, Emma Welsh, Nicole Wise, Steven Young

TRAVERSE THEATRE - BOARD OF DIRECTORS
Chair **Stuart Hepburn**, Secretary **Scott Howard**
Kate Atkinson, Barry Ayre, Geraldine Gammell, Lesley Riddoch

THE JUJU GIRL

by

Aileen Ritchie

in memory of my father

Rev. Alexander Ritchie

Characters

KATE, *a Scot in her mid-twenties recently arrived in Africa*

OZZIE, *a well-travelled Australian backpacker with a zest for adventure*

CATHERINE, *a Scots missionary who has been born and brought up in Rhodesia*

DANIEL, *a quiet, reserved Shona man in his late twenties*

EDDIE, *an upbeat Zambian pilot in his mid-twenties*

ANDREW, *a young Scots minister, recently arrived in Rhodesia with an earnest disposition*

PRECIOUS, *a Shona woman, branded as a witch, living as a servant*

JOSHUA, *a Shona man with leprosy*

MARTHA, *a fifteen-year-old Mozambiquan refugee*

NYANGA, *a witchdoctor*

TRAIN CONDUCTOR, TAXI DRIVER, BEGGAR.

Scene One

A young woman KATE *walks onto the stage alone she is dressed like a backpacker who has been on the road for a while. She turns to the audience.*

KATE. It was hot, very hot. I was in a taxi. An emergency taxi.

She is joined by a number of Africans and a lone Australian male who all squash into the car beside her.

OZZIE. Sorry, cheers – thanks.

KATE. It's what we in Scotland would call an Estate car – seating capacity, six?

OTHERS IN TAXI. Ten.

KATE. It seemed to be held together by scaffolding and sellotape.

DRIVER (*Shona*). Usatuke mota yangu! (Don't insult my car!)

OZZIE. He said you shouldn't insult his car.

KATE. Sorry. Anyway I was in the front . . .

DRIVER. Take the money, eh?

KATE. Which means you get to be the conductor.

OZZIE. There you go.

KATE. Ta. When . . .

All collectively scream and freeze –

KATE. I was thinking – is this it? Is this my number up, careering through the streets of Harare in a beaten up jalopi and what have I done with my life when . . .

– and are thrown forward. The driver swears in Shona.

DRIVER. Voetsek!

The car comes to a halt.

ALL. Phew.

They all laugh nervously with relief.

DRIVER. Okay?

KATE. Sure. I think I'll get out here.

DRIVER. This is the station.

The people of the taxi disperse.

OZZIE. Quite a buzz eh?

KATE. Sorry?

OZZIE. Near death experiences – kind of like the rush you get going off the Vic Falls bridge. Aaaaaaah! Mental.

KATE. I could have done without it.

OZZIE. Still someone up there is watching out for you, eh? Been white water rafting yet?

KATE. No.

OZZIE. Man, don't miss that. I got thrown out on the fifth – was under for best part of a minute. Bet I'll have bilharzia or some other shit.

KATE. I'm not into thrill seeking.

OZZIE. C'mon.

KATE. I'm not one for the tourist traps. I'd like to find the real Africa.

OZZIE. Don't tell me you're into the witchcraft and juju.

KATE. I keep an open mind.

OZZIE. Now that's scary. Next you'll be coming to Oz to hang out with the aboes.

KATE. Are you getting the train?

OZZIE. No, I'm off to a backpacker's lodge – they've got hot water, Australian beer and a guy who beats his head with a tray to the tune of Killer Queen. Now that I've got to see.

KATE. Nice to meet you.

OZZIE. Yeah, we'll catch up with each other. Your train awaits. And remember, never trust the natives.

There is an explosion of sound – people shouting in different languages, calling to each other – a sense of urgency to it all. The stage is piled with old luggage by two young African men. The luggage becomes a seating bank and the space becomes a railway carriage.

The shouting and calling subsides leaving the hiss and hum of the steam locomotive. It becomes louder and more insistent as it heats up to leave.

A young woman appears. This is CATHERINE. She perches on the luggage in a genteel fashion and reads from her diary.

Scene Two

CATHERINE. My journey from our mission station to Salisbury on Rhodesian Railways is proving a most pleasant experience. I have been afforded all the luxuries that civilised life can offer, while enjoying the spectacular vistas of the African bush or 'bundu' as the natives call it. The sunset was quite breath taking and the roast beef quite palatable. There is something reassuring about retiring for the night and finding freshly laundered linen on the bed. These touches quell the slight anxiety of what lies ahead on my arrival. I only hope that I have chosen well.

Scene Three

A young African woman starts singing a soulful, heartfelt wailing lament (which sounds like a hymn) and rattles change in a metal plate.

There is frenetic activity around the train. People move to and fro, randomly at first, then blending into a choreographed tide moving up and down. The group breaks in two – one set becomes the travellers, the others the traders. African women put large enamel bowls on their heads and sell brightly coloured ice poles or hard-boiled eggs. The travellers from their position of superiority on top on the travel trunks, call and whistle negotiating price and quality as they haggle loudly with the street traders.

Two people argue heatedly in Shona, then laugh then go back to argument.

A Shona man in his late twenties sits alone with a large bag at his feet. KATE *is walking along outside the train, checking the compartments as she goes. He is hanging out of he window watching the hubbub of activity and enjoying himself.*

KATE *looks hot and weary.*

KATE. Is this 498?

DANIEL. Could be. Numbers at the end there.

He indicates further down. She checks, then gets on the train. He turns to find her at the door of the compartment.

KATE. This is G2.

DANIEL. Mm. Yah. Yah, it is.

KATE. Oh. There must be some mistake. I'll go and get the guard.

DANIEL. What's up?

KATE. Well, I reserved a single coupé. See?

She shows him the ticket.

KATE. I mean I wouldn't mind but they do charge extra.

DANIEL. No problem. I'll move.

KATE. But your ticket . . . if it . . .

DANIEL. It's okay. I don't have one.

He makes no attempt to move.

KATE. Oh.

KATE *watches him and begins to feel anxious.*

KATE. So what's happening here? Do I have to get the guard or what?

DANIEL. He'll come soon. Check your booking. Then I'll buy a ticket and he'll put me some place that's empty. Okay?

KATE *feels defensive, unconvinced.*

KATE. Okay.

DANIEL. You want a Fanta?

He unzips his bag and pulls out a bottle of orange. He puts it to his face to feel the glass and smiles.

DANIEL. It's cold.

KATE. No. Thanks.

KATE is still standing and the panic which is rising in her is growingly apparent. DANIEL is the opposite – he prises the bottle top off with his teeth and takes a long slug. He gets pleasure from the cooling effect and visibly relaxes.

KATE. Right, all I've got is 60c. Take it and find another seat.

DANIEL. No. Thanks.

KATE. It's all you're going to get.

DANIEL. I don't want it.

KATE. Look, don't take this personally but I've had nothing but hassle off . . . wide boys . . . crooks.

DANIEL. We call them tsotsies

KATE. Tsotsies then since I've arrived. Trying to sell me 'genuine' emeralds, change money on the black market, help pay for some guy's mother's operation. Last two days I was so fed up all I did was watch CNN in my hotel.

DANIEL. Where were you staying?

KATE. The Sheraton.

DANIEL. Nice.

KATE. Safe.

DANIEL. You know what tsotsies call you people?

KATE. No.

DANIEL. Mhene. It means game. You guys hunt the big five. The tsotsies hunt the big tourist.

KATE. Is that meant to be funny?

KATE is feeling increasingly defensive but DANIEL shrugs and smiles.

DANIEL. This is life here, my friend. This is Africa.

Scene Four

Salisbury railway station. Waiting. A white man of about thirty in clerical collar stands rigidly staring ahead of him, lost in thought. ANDREW is praying to himself.

ANDREW. Well this is it Lord, this is Africa. Please let this be the right vocation for me in life. Let this day mark a new beginning . . .

He does not see CATHERINE. She takes a deep breath, steps forward and speaks. There is a nervous edge to her voice.

CATHERINE. Andrew McPherson I take it?

ANDREW. And you're Catherine. Catherine McLean. Yes! I see the resemblance.

They shake hands formally. ANDREW is very jumpy and enthusiastic. CATHERINE is nervous but displays a sense of humour about the awkwardness of the situation.

CATHERINE. Please don't say that. I think all girls hope to take after their mother.

ANDREW. I'm a great admirer of your father's work here.

CATHERINE. I have gathered that. Sadly I am not my father.

ANDREW. No. You received my letters then.

CATHERINE. Certainly. Thank you.

ANDREW. And thank you. Comfortable journey?

CATHERINE. Fine. I was sorry not to be here to meet you. It seems a little unfair as . . .

ANDREW. I'm the stranger. Yes. It's all a bit different to Edinburgh.

CATHERINE. And this is Salisbury. The city. Wait till you reach the bush.

ANDREW. I'm sure. All very . . . different.

CATHERINE. Yes. I'm sure Scotland would be the same for me.

ANDREW. You've never . . .

CATHERINE. Born and raised here.

ANDREW. That's impressive.

She laughs at his earnestness.

CATHERINE. Not to me. I had no choice in the matter. What now?

ANDREW. The train leaves at six I think.

CATHERINE. But do you want to rest?

ANDREW. No, no. I'd like to take in the sights – if you'd care to show me round.

CATHERINE. I'm not the best guide to Salisbury but I'll do my best.

ANDREW. Shall we?

He offers her his arm to take rather stiffly. She suppresses a smile.

CATHERINE. Will I do?

He is taken off guard by such a direct comment but knows exactly what she means.

ANDREW. Indeed. Aye. Most acceptable.

They walk off together.

Scene Five

The RAILWAY CONDUCTOR *appears in the doorway and* KATE *looks visibly relieved.*

CONDUCTOR. Tickets.

KATE. Hold on – here, yes.

CONDUCTOR. You, ticket.

Conversation in Shona:

DANIEL. Imarii? (How much is it?)

CONDUCTOR. Class ipi? (Which class?)

DANIEL. Anoita marii makirasi acho? (How much for which class?)

CONDUCTOR. Haikona kupedza ngura yangu.1st, 2nd, kmama Mbombera (Don't waste my time. 1st, 2nd or economy?)

DANIEL. Mbombera (Economy.)

CONDUCTOR *gives him the ticket and takes the money.* KATE *cannot understand the conversation and looks a little uneasy.*

KATE. Is everything alright?

DANIEL. No problem.

KATE. Excuse me. What time is dinner?

CONDUCTOR. Dinner is off. No chef.

KATE. But it's a twelve hour journey. What am I meant to do?

CONDUCTOR. Go to sleep.

KATE. Can you believe that?

CONDUCTOR. Keep the window shut.

KATE. But it's so hot.

CONDUCTOR. The tsotsies will come. You'll be crying in Bulawayo.

The CONDUCTOR *leaves.*

KATE. This is a nightmare.

DANIEL. Next time – you'd best fly.

KATE. No food, half a bottle of water. And what happens when I go to the bathroom? Can I lock my coupé?

DANIEL. No.

KATE. Are you going?

DANIEL *gets to his feet and starts dragging his heavy bag towards the door of the compartment.*

DANIEL. Yes.

KATE. Why?

DANIEL. Because all I was looking for was some peace and quiet. I'm not going to find it here, am I?

KATE. Don't leave. I'm sorry.

DANIEL. Why should I stay?

KATE. Be nice to have a bit of company. Just for a while.

DANIEL. But you don't trust me.

KATE. I didn't say that. I don't know you.

DANIEL. My name is Daniel. Is that enough?

KATE. I'm Kate, short for Katherine.

She puts out her hand. They shake hands. It is a mess as she is doing a formal British handshake and he is doing a Shona handshake.

KATE. Pleased to . . . oops.

DANIEL. Here, may I?

He takes her hand and shows her the three stages of the handshake.

DANIEL. First like this, then this and then this, yes?

They try it and it works, making them laugh.

KATE. Yes. Well here we are then.

DANIEL. Okay?

KATE. Sure.

They rock in rhythmic silence to the motion of the train.

Scene Six

The motion is the same for CATHERINE *and* ANDREW *as they sit opposite each other in their compartment.* ANDREW *is finding it rather hot and is wiping his neck with a linen hanky.*

They are silent. CATHERINE *is watching him intently.*

ANDREW. I'll retire shortly.

CATHERINE. Don't on my account. So soon I mean.

ANDREW *looks out of the window.*

ANDREW. It's not how I imagined.

CATHERINE. In what respect?

ANDREW. The train. It's all so . . . civilised. Leather seats, etched glass, white linen. A real home from home.

CATHERINE. We have a lot to thank Cecil Rhodes for.

ANDREW. Certainly. He seems to have civilised the whole region.

CATHERINE. You sound disappointed.

ANDREW. I was hoping for a real adventure.

CATHERINE. That will come. Enjoy it while you can.

ANDREW. I intend to.

CATHERINE. I do love the place.

ANDREW. And the natives?

CATHERINE. Two main tribes – the Shonas and the Ndbele – the latter very akin to the Zulu warriors. We'll be in the Eastern Highlands with the Shonas. Farming people – we should be alright there.

ANDREW. But the people are welcoming.

CATHERINE. Well, it's hard to say. This is not my home territory. I had hoped to stay nearer to the community I knew, had grown up with, for some moral support but well – it wasn't to be.

ANDREW. But your father will be there.

CATHERINE. He went ahead some weeks ago just as the old minister was about to return to Scotland. He is waiting to see us settled – and to marry us of course. Then he'll go back to his own parish.

ANDREW. Wonderful. With your father behind me, I could not ask for a more solid foundation to start my own ministry.

CATHERINE. It won't be easy.

ANDREW. I don't want it to be easy, Catherine. Certainly not. I hope you will realise that my character is not afraid of hard work.

CATHERINE. I do not doubt the integrity of your 'character' for one moment.

ANDREW. Are you making fun of me?

CATHERINE. Only a little. Is that allowed?

ANDREW. I am in earnest. You must understand that.

CATHERINE. I do, my dear. But we will both need a sense of humour on occasion if we are to manage.

ANDREW. We will manage.

ANDREW looks dour and resolute. CATHERINE sits back in her seat obviously experiencing doubts about her suitor.

Scene Seven

KATE is wiping herself down with a piece of cloth. She is looking in the mirror. She traces the outline etched on the surface of the mirror.

KATE. RR?

DANIEL. Rhodesian Railways.

KATE. Colonialism is everywhere. I'm from Scotland. We were colonised by the English too.

DANIEL. Really. Is Scotland a rich country?

KATE. Not really. Well, I suppose in comparison to here, yes.

DANIEL. It must be. Your ancestors grew rich from our country.

KATE. My ancestors?

DANIEL. Yes. It was the Scottish who colonised us.

KATE. I never knew that. We always think of ourselves as the oppressed, the underdogs.

DANIEL. The white farmers have done well here but now they are crying because we want their land back.

KATE. Well I won't be crying for them.

DANIEL. You don't mind that these people have made a life here, provided employment for thousands of Africans. Now they are being driven out.

KATE. Well that shouldn't happen. That's like ethnic cleansing. Whatever happened before – well, it's in the past isn't it?

DANIEL. Sure. The Scots came here, took the best land and now we plough the poorest soil and our crops are first to fail when the drought comes. Is that fair?

KATE. No. I'm not trying to defend them. I only want what's right.

DANIEL. So do I.

Silence.

KATE. It's so hot.

DANIEL. No. You should visit Kariba. Now that's hot.

KATE. And you should visit Scotland. Now that's cold.

DANIEL. Maybe one day. You have lots of hills and lakes.

KATE. We call them lochs. But not filled with hippos and crocs – only the Loch Ness monster if you believe that.

DANIEL. What's that?

KATE. They say this hump backed creature lives in the loch. There have been sightings and a few dodgy photos but people flock there to see if they can catch a glimpse.

DANIEL. Have you seen it?

KATE. No. I haven't even seen Loch Ness. Have you been to Kariba?

DANIEL. Once.

KATE. I've heard the lake is very beautiful.

DANIEL. It's good for tourism.

KATE. That sounds very negative.

DANIEL. It has been created artificially. They had a lot of trouble building it.

KATE. In what way?

DANIEL. People say the spirits were angry so first of all the dam burst, then some people died in a freak accident. Finally it got so hot there the workmen had to carry their metal tools in buckets of cold water. It went to over 40C.

KATE. Do you believe that? About the spirits?

DANIEL. I believe they had a struggle but rightly so. The Tonga people were cleared from their homeland. It was their farms they flooded to create the dam.

KATE. What do the Tonga do now?

DANIEL. Sell baskets at the roadside.

KATE. Like this one?

KATE shows him a basket she has in her bag.

DANIEL. Nice. Yeah, this is one of theirs.

DANIEL. How much?

KATE. Fifty dollars. God, I feel guilty now.

DANIEL. Don't. You paid them a lot for it.

The train shudders to a halt.

KATE. What's happening?

DANIEL gets up and looks out the window. He shouts down the train and other voices shout out in Shona. There seems to be a heated argument, then things die down again. He goes to get out.

DANIEL. Time for a walk.

KATE. What?

DANIEL. The train is broken down. Best to get off for a while. Think of it as a bush safari.

KATE. No, I'll wait. It won't be long, I'm sure. The Rough Guide says these trains are quite reliable.

DANIEL. Did it? See you later. Keep an eye on my stuff, yeah?

KATE. Yeah.

DANIEL steps down. KATE sits alone looking nervous and extremely hot.

She looks out. The place fills with hot and weary travellers drinking and talking, taking the air. Some sit down, others stretch out weary limbs. It is a relaxed and friendly atmosphere.

EDDIE, a young Zambian man, appears on the scene. His appearance is very American-influenced – baggy jeans, baseball hat and expensive sunglasses. He exudes energy.

DANIEL greets EDDIE who is out taking the air and drinking from a bottle of Castle beer. They greet each other, exchange a Shona handshake.

DANIEL (*Shona*). Hey Eddie, zviri kufamba here? (Hey, Eddie. How is it going?)

EDDIE (*Shona*). Zviri kufamba (Good – hey I was just thinking about you. You were meant to call me.)

DANIEL (*Shona*). Ndanga ndiri kuzokufonera. Asi unoziva kuti hatisi tese tine macellular. Saka howzat? (I was going to do just that. But not all of us have mobiles, you know. How is it with you?)

EDDIE. Sharp.

KATE emerges and joins DANIEL. EDDIE looks at him with a mixture of bewilderment and amusement.

EDDIE. Yo! danny boy, you have been a busy man. Masikati sisi..

KATE. Masikati.

EDDIE. Now this one has a wife – but me, sisi, I'm a free man.

He gives her a Shona handshake and she knows what to do. He notes this.

EDDIE. Ah, this one is one of us eh?

DANIEL. Eddie!

EDDIE. Hey bro – it's no problem. Pleased to make your acquaintance, Mrs. lady.

KATE. Kate.

EDDIE. Beautiful name, beautiful face.

KATE. Thanks. What do you do, Eddie?

EDDIE. I'm a pilot. An airline pilot.

KATE. Really. (*She doesn't believe him.*)

DANIEL. He is.

EDDIE. And you?

KATE. I work for a charity. In Glasgow.

DANIEL. My cousin is a missionary there. In Toryglen. Is that nice?

KATE. Ehm – you want the truth?

She shakes her head.

DANIEL. Yes. He finds it hard I think.

KATE. And you, Daniel?

EDDIE. Oh, this one is a very bad man – the worst kind of tsotsie. He looks so respectable too. But be careful, Kate.

KATE. Is that right?

EDDIE. I'd like to visit Scotland. Celtic Football Club, Rod Stewart, deep-fried Mars Bars – you guys are into some seriously weird culture.

KATE. I've come to Africa to find some real culture. Scotland is a bit limited. All heather and haggis.

EDDIE. There's more than that. Great scenery. I want to swim in a big lake without worrying if a croc will snap me in two.

DANIEL. No, but they have other monsters eh Kate?

KATE. That's right. Nessie might get you instead.

EDDIE *looks at* DANIEL *a little bemused.*

EDDIE. Since when are you the expert?

DANIEL *smiles*.

EDDIE. Still, now I've got a Scottish friend, I won't be short of a bed eh?

KATE. I have a tiny flat.

EDDIE. I take up very little room.

DANIEL. He's teasing you, Kate.

KATE. I know.

EDDIE. Was I now?

DANIEL. I was going to call on you in Bulawayo.

EDDIE. You need a place?

DANIEL. Till tomorrow.

EDDIE. You got it. And you precious? I have a big place – yard, dog, pool.

KATE. I'll be fine. I'll let you to talk to your friend. The sun's a bit much for me.

EDDIE *rolls his eyes at* DANIEL *and smiles*.

EDDIE. Did I come on too strong?

DANIEL. Don't you always?

The two men settle into a jokey conversation in Shona.

KATE goes back up into the compartment. She returns to the guys completely panic-stricken.

KATE. It's gone – my bag has gone.

DANIEL. What?

KATE. Is this another set up? Is that what all this is about? Get me off the train and get your friend to rob me. Well, I . . .

EDDIE. Don't accuse him. He's the last man who would . . .

DANIEL. It's okay, Eddie. She's upset. Hey, Kate – calm down. We aren't your enemy, okay?

KATE. I'll tell you something. I'm going straight to the police at Bulawayo – do you hear me?

EDDIE. Where's your stuff, Daniel?

DANIEL. They took it too.

KATE. They didn't take that.

She points to a large bag.

DANIEL. Pick it up.

KATE. What?

DANIEL. Try.

KATE. Shit! What's in that?

DANIEL. Some stones, that's all. Worth nothing to a tsotsie.

EDDIE. Bet you had plenty good stuff. Sony Walkman, Olympus Trip camera.

KATE. Never mind that – the person must still be on the train – what are you going to do about it?

EDDIE. Okay Daniel – you take first class, I'll do economy. We'll accuse everyone and see who gets punched first.

DANIEL. What would you like us to do, Kate?

KATE. I don't know. I had no right to accuse you. I'm sorry. I'm sorry.

EDDIE. Well sisi, the offer of my bed still stands.

The train whistle goes and the resting passengers get to their feet and move.

Scene Eight

CATHERINE *is carried in a sedan chair by two 'natives'. They move forward with* ANDREW *leading the way.*

CATHERINE. Why don't I come down and walk beside you?

ANDREW. No – you should travel in style and comfort and I should learn to cross this terrain on foot.

CATHERINE. But I would feel better to be in your company.

ANDREW. If you insist.

CATHERINE. I do.

ANDREW. Put her down . . . down I said.

They do so.

CATHERINE. Have you spotted much as you have walked through?

ANDREW. Only kudu and some giraffe.

She emerges from the chair.

ANDREW. Allow me.

He takes her hand and helps her out.

ANDREW. I have read up extensively on the flora and fauna. One can live well from hunting and the vegetation.

CATHERINE. We tend to eat like the natives – sadza, a kind of porridge mixed with nyama, that's meat. It is filling and nutritious but is much simpler than you will be used to.

ANDREW. The cooking at Bible College left much to be desired. Good simple fare well cooked sounds perfect to me.

CATHERINE. My father will be so glad of your company, Andrew. It is years since we have had a visitor from Edinburgh and he has relished the news you have sent him about the Kirk.

ANDREW. I have enjoyed his letters. Ah, I think I see the settlement.

CATHERINE. Yes, but . . .

ANDREW. Here we are. Home sweet home.

CATHERINE. No-one here to greet us. That's odd.

A young Shona woman, PRECIOUS, *comes out. She looks nervously at the ground.*

CATHERINE (*Shona*). Manhera wakadii? (Hello. How are you?)

PRECIOUS (*Shona*). Ndiripo mwakaiiwo (Very well. ma'am.)

CATHERINE (*Shona*). Ko mfundisi Rev. McLean. Vari kupi? (And the minister? Rev. McLean. Is he away?)

PRECIOUS *starts to cry.*

PRECIOUS (*Shona*). No. The pastor has passed away. He got sick three weeks ago and yesterday he died.

ANDREW. What she's saying?

CATHERINE. My father is dead.

ANDREW *goes to* CATHERINE. *She is devoid of emotion. He holds her as the young Shona woman weeps. Those who have carried her in the chair begin to talk quietly among themselves.*

ANDREW. Go inside and lie down.

CATHERINE. No – I must. I don't know what I should do.

ANDREW. You girl, the mistress is in shock. Take her inside.

CATHERINE *allows herself to be taken away passively.*

ANDREW. The rest of you go.

The 'natives' look on unsure what to do.

ANDREW. Go I said.

They disperse and ANDREW *is left alone. He looks about himself, the abandoned sedan chair, the luggage left strewn around. He follows* CATHERINE *inside.*

Scene Nine

EDDIE *is going to the fridge.* KATE *follows a little unsure. She only now has what she is wearing. She helps carry the heavy bag which belongs to* DANIEL.

EDDIE. Welcome to my penthouse batchelor apartment. The coldest beer, the hottest women and the largest satellite dish in Southern Africa. Sisi? (*Shona.*) Uri kupi? (Where are you, eh?)

DANIEL *and* KATE *exchange an amused smile as* EDDIE *goes off to find his housegirl.*

KATE. No wonder they didn't try to steal this.

DANIEL. I agreed to take too much.

*He unzips the bag and takes out something which is
wrapped in a towel. It is a Shona sculpture. It is smooth and
abstract and very beautiful.*

KATE. That's beautiful. This is Shona sculpture, right?

DANIEL. Yes.

KATE. I've been reading about it. The spirit is in the stone and
the sculptor carves out the abstract shape.

DANIEL. I see. Is this an ancient tradition?

KATE. No, Shona sculpture is quite a recent phenomenon it
comes from – you're taking the piss again, aren't you?

DANIEL. No. I'm interested. I didn't know Shona sculpture
was so famous around the world.

KATE. I read up on Zimbabwe before I came.

DANIEL. You'll need to tell me all about it.

KATE. Did you make that?

DANIEL. No, my Uncle. He lives in the township – Glenview –
outside Harare. I'm going to sell these to a shop he supplies.

KATE. You're a good nephew.

DANIEL. My youngest brother lives with them so he can go to
teacher training in Belvedere. We help each other out.

KATE. That's nice.

DANIEL. Don't worry, I'm not about to ask for a contribution
to his education.

KATE. I didn't think you were. Anyway, now I have nothing to
give him. Can I use his phone and then I'll be out of your
way?

DANIEL. Need to get Eddie to take the lock off.

EDDIE *re-enters.*

KATE. The lock?

EDDIE. You know what it's like. You can't trust anyone around
here.

KATE. I'll stop at a hotel overnight and get replacement cheques tomorrow.

DANIEL. Have you got a credit card?

KATE. No.

DANIEL. Then you might find it difficult.

EDDIE. That's right – this is a cash only society.

KATE. Surely any decent hotel would take my word . . .

DANIEL. Would you take mine?

EDDIE. Or mine?

KATE. But you're strangers.

DANIEL. And what are you in our country?

   EDDIE *unlocks the phone.*

EDDIE. Try The Bulawayo Sun. Nearest we have to a Hilton – apart from my place of course. Here, it's ringing.

KATE. Hello? Yes, I'd like a single room with private bathroom – ehm, for tonight maybe longer. Now, I'd not be able to pay for that in advance. No, no credit card – no I've lost my passport too. But I would . . . I see. Thank you.

   She comes off the phone feeling humiliated and alone.

KATE. Okay, you win. They won't take me. I'd appreciate it if I could stay overnight.

EDDIE. Sure princess. You got it.

DANIEL. You'll be okay here, Kate. I promise you.

EDDIE. Don't you have a moneybelt?

KATE. Yeah, I had, a cheap, nylon thing. Felt so horrible against my skin. I ended up putting it in my rucksack. I thought I was going to be safe there – as long as I was with it.

DANIEL. I know. I'm sorry – people, well, we don't have any unemployment, social security – people get desperate.

   A young African girl, MARTHA, *comes through wearing a headscarf and print wraparound. She doesn't look up at* KATE *as she waits for instruction.*

EDDIE. Some drinks eh?

The girl goes off and comes back with a selection of bottles on a tray. KATE tries to smile at her, be friendly. She looks too nervous to respond.

KATE. Is this your little sister?

DANIEL. No, Martha looks after the house for Eddie, don't you?

The girl nods shyly.

EDDIE. Hey, you want a Castle?

EDDIE passes her a beer and cracks one with his teeth.

KATE. Yeah. Thanks. I need it.

EDDIE. And a Fanta for my good friend and chaperone, Daniel.

She looks at the bottle top and seems to be contemplating trying to open it.

EDDIE. Hey, here. (*He does it for her.*) Come out to the stoop – it's cooler.

KATE. Only if Daniel comes too.

EDDIE. Kate, I am not about to pounce. I like to let a woman come to me.

KATE. Don't hold your breath.

Scene Ten

CATHERINE *and* ANDREW *stand over a dirt grave marked with a simple wooden cross.* ANDREW *is finishing a prayer.*

ANDREW. For I am the way, the truth and the life. Teach us by thy holy name, what to believe, what to do and wherein to find our peace. In thine own name sake we ask it. Amen.

PRECIOUS *and* CATHERINE: *to the tune of Amazing Grace.*

They go and sit outside. MARTHA disappears. EDDIE emerges with his ghetto blaster and puts on some rhumba. It has an infectious energy to it.

Scene Eleven

EDDIE, KATE *and* DANIEL *sit on the stoop together.*

EDDIE. Ah, Kanda Bongo Man, my friend – now he knows how to make music.

They listen to the music. EDDIE *gets up with his beer bottle in one hand and dances to it.*

EDDIE. Fantastic eh?

DANIEL. Not to my taste.

KATE. It's quite catchy.

This lack of enthusiasm stops EDDIE *in his tracks.*

EDDIE. Oh thanks. I'm only trying to educate you about the real culture – what the povo like.

KATE. The povo are welcome to it.

EDDIE *and* DANIEL. Oooh!

EDDIE. This one is a townie. Definitely. One tough lady.

EDDIE. Dance with me, Kate.

KATE. No. I'm fine here.

EDDIE. Ah, these whites – scared that they can't move.

KATE. Is that right?

She gets up and dances a little. She moves well. EDDIE *advances to groove with her but she turns and avoids contact.* DANIEL *laughs. She sits down.*

DANIEL. You showed him.

KATE. Do you dance?

EDDIE. That one was the best break dancer in the township.

DANIEL. That was a long time ago.

EDDIE *laughs and pours his beer on the ground.* KATE *looks at what he is doing.*

EDDIE. Doro for the dead.

DANIEL. He's sharing his beer with his ancestral spirits.

KATE *pours a little on the dry earth.*

KATE. For Gran.

DANIEL. Your gran passed away?

KATE. Yes. We were going to come here together. But then she died, quite suddenly so here I am alone.

EDDIE. Was she a beer drinker?

KATE. No, but she liked a drop of whisky.

They laugh together, then fall silent.

EDDIE. Those tsotsies my friend – they're clever.

KATE. Don't remind me.

EDDIE. You insured?

KATE. Yes.

EDDIE. Then everybody wins.

KATE. What?

DANIEL. Ah, Eddie – you're talking like a Zambian now.

EDDIE. Hey, want to change any zim.dollar for kwacha?

DANIEL. No.

EDDIE. No. You seen kwacha? Zambian money? Here.

EDDIE *takes a thick wad of notes out of his back pocket. They are very torn and dirty. He throws them on the ground.*

EDDIE. Good paper to wipe your arse with. People in Zambia can't buy goods unless they get hard currency.

KATE. So stealing all I have is okay?

EDDIE. No, no. That's what you think I'm saying. I'll tell you a story, right?

DANIEL. *Ah ich man.*

EDDIE. No, listen, listen please. This guy is chauffeur right? The boss has a big car, big Mercedes, but the driver, our man, gets badly paid. So this guy says to him, bro you want to make some money, some U.S. dollar man, then park the car at a bottle store, go inside leaving the keys. That's all.

Two minutes. So the man does this and gets paid. The tsotsie gets the car and the company gets the insurance. Who loses?

DANIEL. But he's helped to steal the car.

KATE. And his company . . .

EDDIE *is extremely emphatic.*

EDDIE. The company get the insurance, the boss gets a newer car and the chauffeur is richer for it. Everybody's happy. Cheers!

KATE. But what if the insurance don't pay out and the chauffeur loses his job?

EDDIE. He'll become a tsotsie and steal your bags!

DANIEL. You're impossible.

KATE. That's one word.

EDDIE. Now I don't agree with that kind of corruption. No, no, no.

KATE. No.

EDDIE. I'd like to get myself a white wife, a nice rich white wife.

KATE. Rich rules me out.

DANIEL. Eddie always has a string of women.

EDDIE. I'm a pilot. They like the uniform.

KATE. And your powers of persuasion.

EDDIE. How can you resist?

KATE. Very, very easily.

Scene Twelve

ANDREW *takes her hand as* CATHERINE *looks quite emotional.* ANDREW *seems full of vigour.*

CATHERINE. I feel very alone.

ANDREW. You have me now.

CATHERINE. Yes.

ANDREW. And Precious. She said she'll stay on, help you about the house.

CATHERINE. Yes.

ANDREW. We vowed we'd make a new life. We have to stick to that.

CATHERINE. Yes.

ANDREW. Your father had a wonderful ministry. But now, well now it's our turn.

CATHERINE. You wrote a lot about my father.

ANDREW. Indeed. Every kirk in Scotland was aware of his work here. Why, at the General Assembly there was a special lecture devoted entirely to the conversion of the dark continent and his mission was named as an outstanding success.

CATHERINE. And you want that too?

ANDREW. Well, I could not presume to . . .

There is a coldness in her manner which we have not seen before.

CATHERINE. No, you could not.

ANDREW. Have I said something to offend you?

CATHERINE. No.

ANDREW. Please, Catherine – we must be honest with each other.

CATHERINE. If you insist.

ANDREW. I do.

CATHERINE. My father and mother came to Africa because they believed that this is the work God wanted them to do. My mother died of malaria five years later. Even though I was only two and everyone advised him to go back, my father kept on. He built a mission, a school and a hospital in ten years. He never once sought fame or favour for it and if you want to follow his example then forget Scotland, the

General Assembly and the Kirk Elders. None of them can help us now.

ANDREW. I understand your loyalty to your father and his memory. It makes me feel humbled to hear you talk the way you do.

CATHERINE. I did not mean to criticise you by comparison.

ANDREW. But how do I prove myself to you, Catherine?

CATHERINE. I am not asking you to do that.

ANDREW. I think you are. I am a stranger in a strange land.

CATHERINE. I know. I am not trying to test you.

ANDREW. No? I think you do. I feel that you are standing back from me to decide whether I am a fit husband or not. That isolates and disappoints me. Your letters were so warm and full of belief and trust. Now I am here, you seem cold and judgmental.

CATHERINE. I feel lost without my father, Andrew. And however much I want to be close to you, you are still a stranger to me and I feel scared to honour our commitment. That is selfish though. I realise that.

ANDREW. I am sure your father gained strength from having you by his side.

CATHERINE. I hope that he did.

ANDREW. Then trust me, give me the strength to carry on his work. If we do not stand together, we will stumble and fail. Together everything is possible.

CATHERINE. You are right. My grief has obscured all else.

ANDREW. I am not a bad or evil man.

CATHERINE. I know that.

ANDREW. As for being romantic – I've never had much experience in these matters. My shyness is not an asset when it comes to matters of the heart.

CATHERINE. I never thought of you as shy.

ANDREW. Desperately so – as a child. In public life, I have managed to overcome it but my private life, well . . .

CATHERINE. You found corresponding easier than encountering me face to face.

ANDREW. Yes. You are not tongue-tied in a letter.

CATHERINE. No. I see that. Oh Andrew, we know so little of each other.

ANDREW. I hope one day, you will love me with the strength and depth of feeling that you have for your father.

CATHERINE. I will try.

ANDREW. Will you embrace me?

CATHERINE. Gladly.

They hug and kiss for the first time.

ANDREW. We must make arrangements to visit another missionary. The sooner we are married, the sooner we can face our future together.

Scene Thirteen

KATE *pours beer on the ground.* EDDIE *is playing pop music in the kitchen. There is the sound of* MARTHA *beating a pot of sadza.* DANIEL *sits next to* KATE. *They seem pensive, close to each other in a way.*

KATE. She died suddenly – in her sleep.

DANIEL. When someone in the township dies, we take all the furniture out the house, take down the curtains and keep on all the lights. The men sit outside by the fire, all night – the women stay together in the house. People come, pay their respects, give money toward the funeral expenses. We grieve together.

KATE. It was raining when they buried her. It poured all day. We had stale sausage rolls in a co-operative function suite. It was all very . . . Scottish.

KATE smiles weakly at her lame attempt at a joke.
DANIEL doesn't laugh.

DANIEL. She was old. That is a comfort.

KATE. Not to me. In her stories she was always young and always here.

DANIEL. Why did she go back to Scotland?

KATE. She would never say.

Silence.

DANIEL. And now abideth faith, hope, love, these three; but the greatest of these is love.

KATE. You're a Christian?

DANIEL. I'm afraid so.

KATE. Why afraid?

DANIEL. Because I don't think we are likely to share that belief.

KATE. Religion – it's all bigotry and hatred in Scotland – Catholic versus Protestant. I have nothing to do with either.

DANIEL. But what do you believe in?

KATE. I'm interested in traditional stuff – witchdoctors, juju – that kind of thing.

He finds this a little amusing.

DANIEL. But not God?

KATE. Not as such, no.

DANIEL. And who do you think the witchdoctor prays to for guidance?

KATE. Well, maybe it's the definition of God that I have a problem with. But well, the missionaries sold you guys down the river, didn't they? Gave you religion and took your land. I mean I admired my gran for having such strong beliefs but she was a product of her time.

DANIEL. Robert Mugabe was educated in a Mission school.

KATE. And?

DANIEL. And now he's the President. So maybe they did something for us, eh?

KATE. That was then – surely things have moved on.

DANIEL. We're above God?

KATE. I didn't say that. But a lot of bad things have been done because of religion.

DANIEL. I agree. But what about faith? So what do you believe in?

KATE. I don't know.

DANIEL. Why did you come to Zimbabwe, Kate?

KATE. To scatter my grandmother's ashes. Her last request and I've messed that up completely. Some tsotsie out there has them.

DANIEL. I'm sorry. Maybe they'll turn up.

KATE. You do have faith, don't you?

DANIEL. Most of the time, Kate. Most of the time.

Scene Fourteen

ANDREW *and* CATHERINE *arrive together as* PRECIOUS *waits for them. They are greeted by a host of villagers all keen to see* CATHERINE *as a new wife. She throws her wedding flowers and* PRECIOUS *catches them. The villagers dance a traditional dance of welcome and the two newly-weds are shown to seats of honour. They are like a king and queen and are obviously very happy.*

ANDREW. I feel like the King of Africa.

CATHERINE. Don't let the tribal chief hear you say that. He will be worried by the competition.

ANDREW. You have made me the happiest man alive.

CATHERINE. No, the happiest husband.

ANDREW. Are you the happiest wife?

CATHERINE. I am.

ANDREW. That is all I want from life, Catherine. To do God's work and make you happy.

CATHERINE. I hope I will prove a good wife and in time, a mother.

PRECIOUS *comes forward and whispers to* CATHERINE.

ANDREW. What is it?

CATHERINE. They want us to dance.

ANDREW. Of course. We could show them a reel or a waltz.

CATHERINE. I can't dance.

ANDREW. What?

CATHERINE. I have never learned. My father was against it. He believed that it was an idle distraction.

ANDREW. But there is nothing better than a good rousing Scottish ceilidh.

CATHERINE. I have never seen one. But I can imagine. You won't get many around here.

ANDREW. Oh yes, we will.

ANDREW goes and produces a stratchy old gramophone record and puts it on. An upbeat Scots tune emanates from it. The crowd wait, expectantly.

ANDREW. May I have the pleasure?

CATHERINE. If you can bear to see me make a fool of myself.

There is applause and excitement as they get into position and wait for the beat. ANDREW *leads* CATHERINE *through a gay gordons. As she gets it, she relaxes and smiles at him.*

CATHERINE. You dance well.

ANDREW. My little sister always begged me to dance with her. She used to stand on my feet and I'd move her round the room.

CATHERINE. What a considerate brother.

ANDREW. And now I'll be a considerate husband.

CATHERINE. I'd like that. I'll try to be a good wife to you, Andrew.

ANDREW. I am fully confident you will. Come on, have a go.

CATHERINE (*Shona*). Huyayi titambe tese.(Come and dance with us.)

The onlookers join in and it becomes like a Scottish ceilidh. The record finishes and the crowd disperse as ANDREW *and* CATHERINE *shake hands with them. Finally they are alone.*

ANDREW. Happy?

CATHERINE. I wish my father had met you, Andrew. He would have been most impressed.

ANDREW. That is a true compliment. We must accept his passing and move on.

CATHERINE. I know that. A boy or a girl ?

ANDREW. What?

CATHERINE. You must have thought about it, surely. I'd like a girl but somehow boys . . . well they seem more robust.

ANDREW. And you?

CATHERINE. I, my dear, have the constitution of an ox.

ANDREW. But not the appearance of one.

CATHERINE. You did it.

ANDREW. What?

CATHERINE. Made a joke.

He looks offended.

ANDREW. I am not totally bereft of a sense of humour.

CATHERINE. Good.

She kisses him.

ANDREW. Boy I think.

CATHERINE. Mmm . . . yes. Called Andrew.

ANDREW. Definitely.

CATHERINE. I hope we are blessed with a happy life.

ANDREW. I was never in any doubt.

CATHERINE. We are in God's hands.

ANDREW. But it is what we do with this opportunity, Catherine. That is how we will be judged.

CATHERINE. Can you leave me, Andrew? I want to prepare myself for bed.

ANDREW. Of course. I will join you, presently.

ANDREW *leaves.*

CATHERINE. Precious?

PRECIOUS *enters.*

PRECIOUS. I am here ma'am.

CATHERINE. Can you help me?

PRECIOUS *brushes her hair and sings a little as she does. They are close and comfortable with each other.*

PRECIOUS. You are a beautiful bride.

CATHERINE. And what do you think of my new husband?

PRECIOUS. You like him?

CATHERINE. He'll do. Yes. I like him.

PRECIOUS. Then I like him too.

CATHERINE. You are allowed to have your own opinion.

PRECIOUS. I know. He is a good dancer.

CATHERINE. He is, isn't he? And kind too.

PRECIOUS. He is pale.

CATHERINE. His health has been a worry in the past. Our correspondence first started when he was convalescing from a long illness. Still, he seems robust now.

PRECIOUS. You will make him strong.

CATHERINE. I hope so. You will stay with us?

PRECIOUS. Yes.

CATHERINE. Will your village ever take you back?

PRECIOUS *shakes her head.*

CATHERINE. Why? I hope you do not mind me prying,
Precious but my father always sought to draw a veil over
things relating to tribalism and witchcraft. But I would like
to know.

PRECIOUS. I was a Nyanga. A healer. A boy was sick in our
village and his mother asked me for help. He died. They say
it was me. I poisoned him.

CATHERINE. And that's when you came to the mission.

PRECIOUS. Yes. I was fourteen. Your father gave me work
and so I stayed. And when he came here to wait for you, he
asked me to come and look after him and then to stay with
you.

CATHERINE. You won't leave us, will you?

PRECIOUS. It was his dying wish that I remain.

CATHERINE. And here you'll stay.

ANDREW. Catherine!

CATHERINE. Thank you, Precious. You may go. Come in,
Andrew.

PRECIOUS *leaves as he enters.*

CATHERINE. What is it you require from your dutiful wife?

ANDREW. I'm going to try my hand at hunting. I want to go
out at first light. Get Precious to arrange some supplies and
two men to accompany me.

CATHERINE. I don't think that's very wise.

ANDREW. No?

CATHERINE. It's very dangerous if you have no real
experience.

ANDREW. Surely it's the only way I'm to gain expertise is to
face these challenges one by one.

CATHERINE. But no-one expects you to be . . .

ANDREW. A good hunter? Perhaps not. And it may be the
very way that I gain respect from these people.

CATHERINE. I think you've gained respect already from your
dancing.

ANDREW. Please, Catherine – don't make fun of me. This is important. They say hunting is the making of a man.

CATHERINE. But you are risking your life and for what?

ANDREW. For our standing in this community. I have no doubt you will relish the task of running things here in my absence. It does seem to be your vocation.

Scene Fifteen

KATE *kneels as* MARTHA *pours water from a kettle over her hands.* DANIEL *indicates to rub her hands under the running water. She wipes her hands on a towel.* DANIEL *does the same and then* EDDIE *lifts the lids off two pots – one of sadza and one of stew.* MARTHA *takes the bowl and leaves.*

KATE. It smells great. How can I repay you?

EDDIE. U.S. dollars. Rolex. Sony Discman.

DANIEL. You eat sadza?

KATE. I'll eat anything. Gladly.

They are about to dig in when DANIEL *indicates to* EDDIE *to stop. He does so, reluctantly.*

EDDIE. Okay, minister – do your worst.

KATE. Minister?

EDDIE. Ah Daniel – what have you been saying?

DANIEL. Nothing. She never asked.

KATE. I thought you sold things – the sculptures.

DANIEL. And I do – for my Uncle. I don't take commission.

KATE. Why didn't you say?

DANIEL. Being a tsotsie was bad enough in your eyes but can you tell me you'd have wanted to spend a twelve hour train journey with a preacher?

KATE. Perhaps. You don't look like the type to press me to convert.

EDDIE. There are some people who he doesn't bother trying to save. Like me. His best friend. The two of us were known to every Shebeen Queen in Bulawayo then he finds God and loses all his old friends. He left me behind. No wonder I drink.

DANIEL. Shall we say grace?

EDDIE. Yea, let us give thanks for this feast – courtesy of me and my big bank balance.

They bow their heads in prayer.

DANIEL. We give thanks for the food before us. Grant us thy blessing Lord for these mercies for Christ's sake, Amen.

EDDIE. Good and short. You must be hungry.

KATE. Amen.

EDDIE. Here. Like this.

He tears a little piece of sadza and rolls it into a ball with his fingers, dips it in the stew and eats it. KATE copies him.

KATE. Where's your friend?

EDDIE. What friend?

DANIEL. She means your maid. Martha eats in the kitchen.

EDDIE. That one is a good worker. She does everything except scrub my back – that's for you to do, Kate.

KATE. I'd rather wash the dishes.

EDDIE. You married then?

KATE. No.

EDDIE. Got a boyfriend?

KATE shakes her head.

EDDIE. Want one?

KATE. What is this?

DANIEL. Please excuse this Casanova.

KATE. What about you, Eddie. Wife, girlfriend, mistress?

DANIEL. All three.

EDDIE. Ah, these townie girls are all the same. It's not you they are after. It's the keys of your Benz, my friend. No, when the time is right I'll settle with a girl from my village and we'll farm in the rurals and be happy.

DANIEL. Hah!

KATE. You're quite a storyteller.

DANIEL. Ah, this one is crazy. He'll live in Borrowdale with a Harare model and drink cocktails by the pool.

EDDIE. Or chubuku in the shebeen. Maybe I'll do both.

DANIEL. And you?

KATE. I'm a free woman.

DANIEL. Like Eddie.

KATE. No. I'm not looking for a relationship. I split up with someone recently. He wasn't the right guy. It took me a long time to realise that.

EDDIE. So you'd like a husband.

KATE. No. I'd like to be with someone who treats me like a human being.

EDDIE. Not a husband then.

DANIEL. We'd all like to be treated well, Kate.

KATE *begins to feel unwell but is fighting it.*

KATE. I'm sorry I was so . . .

DANIEL. Sceptical.

KATE. Rude – on the train. It's just . . .

DANIEL. No, you're right. Look at this one.

EDDIE. Hey!

KATE. I'm sorry. I don't feel so good. I think I need to lie down.

EDDIE. Malaria.

DANIEL. Exhaustion.

EDDIE. No, something contagious – what vaccinations did you have?

KATE. Is there somewhere I can sleep?

EDDIE. Martha has made up the spare room.

DANIEL. I'm sure you'll feel better in the morning.

KATE. I hope so.

DANIEL. I'll wake you early.

KATE. Thanks.

She leaves.

EDDIE. Sure. Sweet dreams sisi. I know what I'll be dreaming of.

Scene Sixteen

CATHERINE *and* PRECIOUS *kneel over* JOSHUA, *a young Shona man in his early twenties.*

CATHERINE. Where did you find him?

PRECIOUS. By the kraal. He is very weak.

CATHERINE. He looks so thin. He is a leper. Look at his hands and feet.

PRECIOUS. You should leave him to me.

CATHERINE. Why?

PRECIOUS. He has a bad fever. You might get disease from him. Then the master will be angry with me for letting you treat him.

CATHERINE. Nonsense. I am not afraid of leprosy. My mother treated lepers. It is not contagious. What is that?

She indicates the little bag which is round his neck like a talisman.

PRECIOUS. Don't touch it.

CATHERINE. Why?

PRECIOUS. It's juju.

CATHERINE. What?

PRECIOUS. Herbs and bones to ward off evil spirits. Leave him to me, please. It's better I'm telling you. His fever is bad.

CATHERINE. Why are you so afraid for me?

PRECIOUS. I have to look after you. Protect you.

CATHERINE. I think we have to look after each other. Don't you agree?

PRECIOUS *nods her head.*

CATHERINE. Get help to bring him to the shed by the house.

PRECIOUS. You should not do this. You cannot help him. If he dies, people will believe you have killed him. They could turn against you – you are a stranger here.

CATHERINE. But it is our Christian duty to help him.

PRECIOUS. He might be possessed. With an evil spirit.

CATHERINE. That is superstition and you know it. God will protect us from evil. We will nurse him and make him well.

PRECIOUS. And what if his fever spreads?

CATHERINE. We'll need to pray that it won't.

PRECIOUS. I have something to cure him. I know it will work.

CATHERINE. You know I can't allow that. The minister would be very angry.

PRECIOUS. Without it, he will die. Look at him.

CATHERINE. Don't ask me to agree to this, Precious.

PRECIOUS. I ask you to trust me, madam. They are only herbs. Good medicine.

CATHERINE. This is between us, yes?

PRECIOUS *nods.*

CATHERINE. Then do what you must.

Scene Seventeen

The drumming starts. It becomes louder and more confident.

KATE *and* CATHERINE. No sleep tonight. In the morning I'll feel safer. Everything will be alright. Joy cometh in the morning.

PRECIOUS *sings a hymn in Shona.*

JOSHUA (*Shona*). Ndiwe ani? (Who are you?)

CATHERINE. It's alright – you are among friends.

KATE. I couldn't sleep.

DANIEL. Neither could I.

PRECIOUS. You had a fever but you're better now.

CATHERINE *and* DANIEL. Take this.

JOSHUA *and* KATE. What is it?

CATHERINE *and* DANIEL. Medicine.

PRECIOUS. Juju.

CATHERINE. Medicine.

KATE *and* JOSHUA. Tatenda.

DANIEL. It'll help you sleep.

KATE. It's the malaria tablets. They give me such nightmares.

PRECIOUS. You should sleep now. I'll sit with him.

CATHERINE *and* DANIEL. Things will seem better in the morning.

Scene Eighteen

The drum beats again. It is slow and rhythmic like a heartbeat. It seems to call out to the spirits who appear in highly painted masks and grass skirts. Their masks seem devilish and frightening. They rattle seed pods and threaten each other. They wear rattles on their legs and stomp hard on the red earth. The sleeping characters sleep. The drumming becomes more insistent, more frenetic – the movement of these whirling demons more anarchic and eventually climaxes. Suddenly, as quickly as they appeared, the demons disappear and the light of morning begins to break.

Interval.

Scene Nineteen

KATE, *in her night attire goes into the kitchen in the dark and trips over something. She puts on the light to reveal MARTHA lying there on a rush mat curled up on the floor. The girl gets to her feet quickly, looking embarrassed.*

KATE. I'm sorry. I didn't know . . .

MARTHA (*Shona*). Sorry.

   KATE *starts hitting the floor with her foot to make them scuttle off.*

KATE. How can you sleep here? Shit, look at those cockroaches!

   DANIEL *comes in to see what the commotion is.* MARTHA *is standing looking down at the floor like she has been caught doing something wrong.*

DANIEL. It's okay, Martha.(*Shona*.) Kate arikuda mvura (Kate wants some water.)

   MARTHA *goes to get some from the fridge.*

KATE. No, it's okay. I'll do it for myself.

   There is an edge to KATE*'s voice.* DANIEL *speaks to* MARTHA *quietly.*

DANIEL (*Shona*). Martha, chimboenda ku sitting room. (Martha, why don't you go to the living room eh?)

   She goes out the room.

KATE. What is she doing, lying there?

DANIEL. It's where she sleeps.

KATE. Sorry?

DANIEL. It is where she sleeps.

KATE. And this guy Eddie – he's meant to be a friend of yours. Does he call himself a Christian too?

DANIEL. No, Eddie and you have much in common – he likes tradition.

KATE. Is it tradition to exploit people? I might have expected this from some Rhodie's but you guys . . .

She runs out of steam lost for words and full of righteous indignation.

DANIEL. He's given her a job, wages, a roof over her head

KATE. Oh yeah, be a skivvy and lie on the floor – what a Christian act.

DANIEL. She's fifteen, a Mozambiquan refugee. She shouldn't even be in Zimbabwe. It might not be luxury to you but she's doing okay.

KATE. You might think so – all I see is exploitation.

DANIEL. No, being on the street as a prostitute – that is exploitation. This is a decent girl trying to live a decent life against all the odds.

KATE. So you're saying this is fine.

DANIEL. No. But the world is full of injustice. Maybe the poverty here is clearer to you. You are travelling, mixing with all kinds of people seeing all kinds of things. If I went as a tourist through Glasgow – seeing it all with fresh eyes – what would I see?

KATE. But it is me who is here. I can't stand it. It makes me feel so guilty.

DANIEL. And I thought you were worried for Martha.

KATE. I am.

DANIEL. She is sleeping in the lounge now. You can rest and not feel guilty. We'll talk tomorrow.

KATE. Fine.

There is darkness and a slow lullaby sung in Shona by PRECIOUS. *As she lies there,* KATE *sings the same hymn as* PRECIOUS *has sung to comfort herself. The two songs draw to a close together and there is no light at all.*

Scene Twenty

JOSHUA *wakes to find* PRECIOUS *by his side.*

JOSHUA. Hello sister.

PRECIOUS. Feeling better?

JOSHUA. Where am I?

PRECIOUS. Close to Nyanga village.

JOSHUA. Are you not afraid of me?

This makes PRECIOUS *laugh.*

PRECIOUS. No, maybe you should be afraid of me. People say I am a witch.

JOSHUA. Now, did you give me something in the night? A love potion perhaps? What Juju have you used on me?

PRECIOUS. I have not need of such things. Anyway, I want to be a Christian now. If I need something to come true, I pray for it.

JOSHUA. I see. Well, my fever has passed. Who do I thank – you or God?

PRECIOUS. Both of us.

They laugh. Suddenly ANDREW*'s voice booms out and the atmosphere changes.*

ANDREW. Precious – the mistress needs you inside.

She immediately gets to her feet and casts her eyes downward, her relaxed and carefree manner has evaporated.

ANDREW. Precious! Who are you?

JOSHUA *lies there and looks at* ANDREW *but does not speak.*

ANDREW. I asked you a question, boy.

PRECIOUS. He cannot speak, Sir. He is too weak from a fever. Your wife told me to take care of him.

ANDREW. Very well then. But don't let it interfere with your other duties. There is much to do, much to do.

ANDREW *strides off and* JOSHUA *looks at* PRECIOUS *in disbelief.*

JOSHUA. You work for him?

PRECIOUS. I work for his wife. I have to make the best of what little I have here. You must understand that.

JOSHUA. Well I will lie here and be very quiet. I am too weak to speak.

PRECIOUS. Good.

PRECIOUS *walks off with a spring in her step.* JOSHUA *lies watching her, smiling.*

Scene Twenty-One

EDDIE *taps the door, respectfully before coming in.* EDDIE *is less showy and more gentle in his manner. It cuts no ice with* KATE *at all who is cold but polite.*

EDDIE. You sleep okay?

KATE (*obviously lying*). Yeah.

EDDIE. Me? I can sleep anywhere.

KATE. I imagine you've had plenty of practice. What time do the banks open?

EDDIE. Eight.

KATE. Good.

EDDIE. You want some tea?

DANIEL. Here, I've got it.

DANIEL *brings in a tray with a metal teapot and a large plate of bread and butter.*

DANIEL. This was all I could find.

KATE. Where's Martha?

DANIEL. She's run to the store to get some eggs.

EDDIE. Oh yes, our guest must have a full English breakfast.

KATE. Don't bother. I never eat in the morning.

DANIEL. You think I made this specially for him?

EDDIE. Come on, sisi. You think my food is bad?

KATE. I didn't say that. I don't want to take any more of your hospitality – that's all. You've done quite enough.

EDDIE. Oh, this one is frosty this morning! Daniel – you weren't sleepwalking last night, were you?

KATE. He certainly was not!

EDDIE. Ah, ah, ah! Something's cooking here. I can smell it, I can taste it,

KATE. Eddie, leave it, will you?

EDDIE. Sure. I know my place.

DANIEL. I'll take you to the Zimbank before I go.

KATE. I can go myself – just point me in the right direction.

DANIEL. No, it's fine. I'll take you. It's on my way.

EDDIE. Where are you bound for, sisi?

KATE. I'm going back to Harare.

DANIEL. Why?

KATE. I'm sick of all this.

EDDIE. All what?

KATE. This – beggars, thieves, refugees on the floor.

DANIEL. She found Martha sleeping by the fridge.

EDDIE. And that's your problem? You white liberals – you're the worst.

KATE. Really. Look, it's your home – obviously you do what you like, who am I to judge?

EDDIE. I like people who know who they are. Atheists are good. They don't believe in nothing and I like that – they've made up their mind. And racists too – you know where you stand with a racist but these white liberals? They say what they think is the right thing to say – not what they believe. They're so afraid of offending somebody that they're scared to have an opinion.

KATE. I'm not scared.

EDDIE. No?

DANIEL. Eddie, leave it – she's not scared. Leave it at that. Let her go.

EDDIE. Sure. So what do you tell your friends back home. Zimbabwe? Naw, give it a miss. They seem okay but those Africans, you can't trust them.

DANIEL. She's not insulting you.

EDDIE. No? Martha on the floor? That's your big problem, yeah?

KATE. I wasn't going to mention it but yes.

EDDIE. How many homeless live in your house?

    KATE *laughs with derision at this line of questioning.*

KATE. Come on.

EDDIE. No, how many?

KATE. When I'm in Glasgow I buy The Big Issue.

EDDIE. What's that?

KATE. A magazine – helping the homeless to help themselves, not exploiting them as child labour.

EDDIE. Maybe Martha should be a tsotsie, is that a better option than her relying on me?

KATE. I'm not saying that. You take everything I say and twist it.

DANIEL. Why do you need our approval?

EDDIE. Sure. What does it matter what we think?

KATE. It doesn't. I can see you think I'm a stupid naive white tourist. I appreciate you helping me out yesterday but now I'll go to the police, report the theft and get the next train back to Harare. That's best all round.

EDDIE. But you've still no money.

DANIEL. And it might be a few days before someone hands something into the police.

KATE. I'm only reporting it for the insurance. I don't expect anything to turn up.

DANIEL. You never know.

EDDIE. Daniel – come on.

DANIEL. She was carrying her grandmother's ashes. I can't see a tsotsie wanting those.

EDDIE. I'm sorry. I didn't know.

KATE. That's why I came to Zimbabwe. I was going to bury them at her mission station in Nyanga. And now, well I don't know what to do.

DANIEL. You could visit the Falls. Everyone should do that.

KATE. Yes, Gran visited there. She loved it.

DANIEL. That's where I'm going – only for a night. I was going on the train but if Eddie got his Benz out the garage.

KATE. You have a Benz and travel by train?

EDDIE. I don't take it to Harare. I don't trust those people or those roads.

DANIEL. You want to take us, Eddie?

EDDIE. No, I want to stay home, drink beer and watch MTV but what the hell. But I'm not taking my car. No way. I'll borrow my girlfriend's car. She can refuse me nothing.

KATE. I couldn't ask that.

EDDIE. You're not asking. We are telling. It's our Christian duty, eh bro?

DANIEL. My first convert.

EDDIE. For today only. Let's have breakfast, then do the police and the bank on the way out of town.

KATE. If you're sure. Then thank you – that'd be great.

MARTHA *comes back with eggs in a brown bag.*

KATE. Can I help you in the kitchen?

> MARTHA *looks at* EDDIE *who merely shrugs.*

EDDIE. Hey, if she wants to work – why not? It's good practice for when she marries me.

Scene Twenty-Two

JOSHUA *is lying asleep.* CATHERINE *and* PRECIOUS *have finished tending his wounds and talk in soft voices by the bottom of his makeshift bed.*

CATHERINE. He is looking much stronger.

PRECIOUS. I know. He sleeps easy now. And he eats. A lot.

CATHERINE. Has he told you anything? About what happened to him?

PRECIOUS. He was cast out of his village. They were scared of his illness. But you are not.

CATHERINE. That is why we are here, Precious. You see that? God has sent us here to help this man and people like him. With your help, we can save many more.

PRECIOUS. Your God is very kind. But he will not believe. He wears bad juju, sisi. He will never give that up.

CATHERINE. All we can do is show him love and compassion. The rest is up to him.

PRECIOUS. I will do all I can.

CATHERINE. Precious – you won't give him any more of your own medicines, will you?

PRECIOUS. No.

CATHERINE. You promise?

PRECIOUS. He is getting better. You do not need my traditional remedies, any more. Neither do I. God will protect me.

CATHERINE. Do you mean that – in your heart?

PRECIOUS. Yes.

CATHERINE *embraces her.*

CATHERINE. What would I do without you?

PRECIOUS. You have a husband. You are lucky.

CATHERINE. Yes. I know.

PRECIOUS. Your father would be proud of you.

CATHERINE. Thank you.

CATHERINE *gets up and leaves* JOSHUA *and* PRECIOUS *alone. He opens his eyes.*

JOSHUA. Now, I understand a little better.

PRECIOUS. Her father was very good to me. When I was thrown out of my village, I thought I would die. Then someone said, go to him, explain. I thought because it was witchcraft he would turn me away but he never turned anyone away, even those who stole from him or used him. He accepted everyone. We loved him.

JOSHUA. Not like this master.

PRECIOUS. I do not think of him as my master, only of my mistress. I cannot leave her.

JOSHUA. Don't believe that they are your salvation. You have saved yourself. You are a strong woman. Believe in that.

PRECIOUS. And you, where will you go when you are well again?

JOSHUA. I thought I was welcome here.

PRECIOUS. You are.

JOSHUA. Good. There is nowhere else I want to be.

Scene Twenty-Three

KATE *and* MARTHA *stand together by the sink. They are washing up together in silence.* KATE *looks at her and smiles trying to break the ice a little.*

KATE. You are from Mozambique?

MARTHA *nods.*

MARTHA (*Portugese*). Sim (Yes.)

KATE. You understand English?

MARTHA *indicates a little.*

MARTHA (*Portugese*). Umpoku. (A little.)

KATE. I am sorry about . . .

KATE *indicates the floor and sleeping.* MARTHA *shakes her head and smiles.*

KATE. Eddie, he is . . . okay? Nice boss?

MARTHA *nods enthusiatically.*

KATE. Good.

They continue drying the dishes.

KATE. Will you go back one day? To Mozambique?

MARTHA *shakes her head.*

KATE. Would you like to? If you had money?

MARTHA *shakes her head.*

KATE. But your family . . . your mother and father?

MARTHA *indicates that they are dead.*

MARTHA. (*Portugese*). Minha familia es morreu. (My family is dead.)

KATE. So here this is good, yeah?

MARTHA *nods.*

MARTHA (*Portugese*). Sim. (Yes.)

KATE. Good.

KATE *looks a little embarrassed as she carries on with the dishes.* DANIEL *joins them.*

KATE. I thought this was woman's work.

MARTHA *speaks to* DANIEL *in Portuguese and* DANIEL *translates into English.*

MARTHA. Ela tem uma fillia pra casa dela? (Ask the lady if she has a housegirl at home?)

DANIEL. She wants to know if you have a maid in Scotland.

KATE. Tell her no. I live alone, look after myself.

MARTHA. Dis qu'ela si eu pode traballhu pra ella. (Ask her if I can come and work for her.)

DANIEL. Martha would like to know if you would want her to come to Scotland to look after your house for you.

KATE. Tell her, she's very kind but no, that's not possible.

MARTHA. Ah sim. En intende. (I understand.)

DANIEL. She says that's okay – she understands.

KATE. I'm sorry.

DANIEL. It's hard isn't it?

KATE. Things are very different here.

DANIEL. And this is the city. The rural is much harder. Your grandmother must have been a very strong woman.

KATE. More than I realised.

DANIEL. Maybe you have inherited that strength.

KATE. I hope so. Can I ask one more favour? This is the last I promise.

DANIEL. What?

KATE. Can we take Martha to the Falls with us?

MARTHA *looks happy at this prospect.*

KATE. Please.

MARTHA. Please.

DANIEL. It's not me you need to convince.

Scene Twenty-Four

PRECIOUS *and* JOSHUA *are sitting together husking peanuts in a big tray.* CATHERINE *is watching them as they laugh and joke together.*

CATHERINE. This is the beginning of our Christian family now. We all need each other and gather our strength from sharing. But where is Andrew in all this, Lord. Where is my husband?

ANDREW. I killed an elephant.

CATHERINE. Really.

CATHERINE *goes to join* JOSHUA *and* PRECIOUS. *She methodically husks peanuts as* ANDREW *talks.*

ANDREW. The biggest bull elephant you have ever seen in your life. There it was, charging towards me, ears flapping but I stood my ground. Then I blasted him. Right between the eyes. He crashed to the ground and suddenly after all that thrashing about – total silence. My heart was pounding like a drum and I felt so . . . so . . . alive. I am going to write about it in the book I am going to publish on Christian Witness.

CATHERINE. Do we have work for Joshua?

ANDREW. Joshua.

CATHERINE. It's his Christian name.

ANDREW. Did you baptise him?

CATHERINE. Of course not. Only you can do that. He doesn't speak, we need to call him something and I thought you'd prefer a biblical name.

ANDREW. Whatever you think appropriate. We pursued the beast right across the lowvelt. It's quite incredible – I was probably the first white man to see any of that landscape.

CATHERINE. Really.

ANDREW. You've hardly listened to a word I've said.

CATHERINE. And you seem to have lost all sense that there is work which we must do and quickly. The rains will come and soon.

ANDREW. I know, I know.

CATHERINE. If you know then why don't you do something about it? The roof isn't finished on the church and if the rains come now then the whole thing will be washed away. I think Joshua should work on that, in fact I have told him that . . .

ANDREW. Who are you to have told anything to anyone?

CATHERINE. I am your wife and . . .

ANDREW. You are my wife and I am tired of being told by you what my ministry should be about.

CATHERINE. How many converts, Andrew?

ANDREW. What?

CATHERINE. How many converts to Christianity? Since we took over here. None. And you dare to compare yourself to my father.

PRECIOUS (*Shona*). Takuanda kunogadzira chikafu chemanheru. (We will go and start cooking for tonight.)

CATHERINE (*Shona*). Ehe. Itai izovozvo. Ndirikuuyaok iyezvino. (Yes. Do that. I will be there in a moment.)

ANDREW. Stop it.

CATHERINE. Go Precious.

ANDREW. Stop it, I said. I forbid you to speak in that heathen language ever again.

CATHERINE. Why is this such a battle between us? If you'd only . . .

ANDREW. You told me I am not your father. Well, that's true. He might have indulged you, Catherine, but no, I'm not going to do that. You are a woman of little education. One thing you lack is a sense of your place. It is to support me – not to guide me or tell me what to do. I have the degree in theology. I have the vocation to this work. Learn from me, Catherine, how to behave, for the day will come when we will return to Scotland and then in my society you will be totally lost.

CATHERINE. Go back to Scotland?

ANDREW. Of course. Once my reputation is sufficient, I could command a major kirk. St. Machars Cathedral, Aberdeen, Trinity South in Edinburgh or even The Barony in Glasgow. I could be the Moderator of the General Assembly by the time I was fifty.

CATHERINE. I thought you wanted to make a life here. Our correspondence suggested . . .

ANDREW. It suggested that my coming here would be desperately needed and that I would be an esteemed and valued member of the religious community. Instead I find that we are stuck in isolation in a Godforsaken place where few will know or care about what we do.

CATHERINE. But maybe that is your vocation. Not to seek high office or court the attention of the kirk establishment but to make a good humble base of Christian hope in an area steeped in tribalism and superstition.

ANDREW. And that is meant to be the sum of my life's work?

CATHERINE. Perhaps your ambitions are unrealistic.

ANDREW. I had romantic notions – I'm the first to admit it.

CATHERINE. And now you've changed your mind?

ANDREW. We'll need to see how our work here progresses, won't we?

CATHERINE. But I thought . . .

ANDREW. You thought you'd find yourself a husband so that your life could go on here as before.

CATHERINE. That isn't true.

ANDREW. No? Then let me lead and learn to follow.

Scene Twenty-Five

DANIEL, KATE, MARTHA *and* EDDIE. EDDIE *and* KATE *are singing along to a song on the radio.* DANIEL *is staring out of the window.*

KATE and EDDIE.
What if God was one of us
Just a slob like all of us
Just a stranger on the bus
Trying to make it home . . .

The song ends and there is a convivial silence as they trundle along till suddenly they go over a particularly big pothole in the road.

ALL. Ah!

EDDIE. This is going to ruin my car.

DANIEL. It's your driving.

EDDIE. It's overloaded. We're scraping the road.

KATE. I appreciate this a lot. Look how happy she is.

MARTHA *gives the thumbs up.*

EDDIE. I'm taking my maid on holiday. I must be out of my mind.

KATE. I thought you said your girlfriend was going to lend you a car.

EDDIE. Her husband was using it.

DANIEL. How selfish of him.

EDDIE. Don't get me wrong – women are great – but unreliable.

KATE. Whereas you can always be depended on?

EDDIE. It's meeting you, Kate. You've changed me. How about we settle down in Glasgow together?

KATE. Hmm, think I'll pass on that one.

DANIEL. Wise woman.

EDDIE. But the preacher here – if he were a free man?

KATE. What?

EDDIE. You like him?

DANIEL. Eddie!

KATE. He's a married man.

EDDIE. Copout.

KATE. What is this?

DANIEL. Don't ask me.

EDDIE. Would you – you know – really – with a black guy. I mean obviously not me. I'm not asking for me.

DANIEL. Why are you asking then?

EDDIE. I'm curious that's all. Look, I've told you, I'm only the driver here – that's all.

KATE. If I met someone I really liked, I hope their colour wouldn't matter.

DANIEL. Good answer.

EDDIE. Yes. Very . . . diplomatic.

KATE. But you doubt my sincerity.

EDDIE. I disagree – that's all. Mixed relationships. I don't approve.

DANIEL. Here we go.

KATE. Really?

DANIEL. This from the man who was engaged to Miss Sweden.

EDDIE. Yeah. Yeah. I mean I do it. Don't get me wrong. I just don't approve – that's all. But if you guys were to – I'd wish you all the best.

DANIEL. But we're not.

KATE. But thanks for making us all feel uncomfortable.

EDDIE. My pleasure.

Scene Twenty-Six

JOSHUA *lies on his makeshift bed.* PRECIOUS *comes to check on him. She carries a lamp.*

PRECIOUS. Shall I leave you the lamp?

JOSHUA. No.

PRECIOUS. No?

JOSHUA. Do not leave me at all.

PRECIOUS. Ah, this one is feeling much better. He will be leaving very soon I am sure. Back to his wife, his family.

JOSHUA. No. I do not want to leave, Precious. I have no-one. I can leave only if you come with me.

PRECIOUS. Ah, and where would we go? The leper and the witch? What life is there for us?

JOSHUA. We are young. We could farm.

PRECIOUS. This is my life now.

JOSHUA. Ah, the sweet little housegirl who cleans for her master.

PRECIOUS. So I come and cook and clean for you? At least they feed me, give me shelter – maybe you would run away, leave me with a baby.

JOSHUA. Don't trust them before me.

PRECIOUS. Do not make me choose. They will be happy for you to stay.

JOSHUA. Would you be happy if I did?

She shrugs as if non-committal.

PRECIOUS. Maybe somewhere a wife is crying. Maybe she is crying for you.

Scene Twenty-Seven

KATE, DANIEL, EDDIE *and* MARTHA *stand on the bridge and gaze ahead of them. They have to shout to hear themselves above the sound of the rushing water.* MARTHA *hangs on tight to* EDDIE. *She looks nervous and unhappy.*

DANIEL. Mosi-oa-tunya. The smoke that thunders.

KATE. It's incredible.

EDDIE (*irritated*). Martha, it's alright – you're safe.

DANIEL. One of the seven wonders of the world.

KATE. Look, a rainbow.

DANIEL. There's always a rainbow.

KATE. Amazing.

EDDIE. Would you get off me, please?

She breaks her grip and hangs onto the bridge.

EDDIE. Is there a beer garden round here?

KATE *and* DANIEL. Eddie!

EDDIE. What? I'm thirsty. All that water – I'm only human.

DANIEL. Come to the edge – below is what they call boiling point. We can climb down there if you want. There's a path.

KATE. I'm fine here. Martha – are you alright?

MARTHA *shakes her head.*

DANIEL. She seems scared.

EDDIE. Go and wait by the car.

MARTHA *shakes her head and hangs on tight.*

EDDIE. Ah, she's scared the spirits will lure her down.

KATE. Don't worry. You're safe with us. My gran saw this. She said it was one of the most romantic places on earth and she's right.

EDDIE. Daniel, why don't you take a little walk, let Kate and I enjoy the romance of this alone.

KATE. Don't move.

EDDIE. Maybe I should be the one taking the little walk . . .

KATE. Yeah straight forward – keep going.

EDDIE. That's it – I'm out of here. I'll take your little 'friend' here to the car. You'll find me in the nearest shebeen.

He takes MARTHA *off the bridge. She looks relieved to go.*

KATE. Did I offend him?

DANIEL. He's not as tough as he appears.

KATE. He's really nice – a bit much at times.

DANIEL. He's playing with you – but I think he does like you.

KATE. I don't need another ladies man. I left one behind in Glasgow and I am not about to let history repeat.

DANIEL. Eddie wants to settle down, but well let's just say he has had his own disappointment too.

KATE. And you – have you had disappointment?

DANIEL. Why do you ask that?

KATE. I don't know. Something about you.

DANIEL. I think life disappoints me, Kate. Let's leave it at that.

Scene Twenty-Eight

A beer garden in Vic Falls. It is awash with activity and rock music. A chubuku bucket is being passed round the group that EDDIE sits with . He is with OZZIE and a young African woman who looks very 'townie' and sophisticated. MARTHA sits head down by EDDIE. She looks bored.

EDDIE. Hey, here they are – over here.

DANIEL. Are you okay with this?

KATE. Better than a lot of Glasgow pubs. And you?

DANIEL. These places were my second home – I haven't always been a minister you know.

KATE. Feeling better, Martha?

MARTHA *nods.*

EDDIE. She wouldn't sit in the car. She's impossible.

MARTHA *smiles.*

OZZIE. How are you doing?

KATE. Hello again.

EDDIE. You guys know each other?

OZZIE. We nearly crashed with this mad ET driver back in Harare.

KATE. Recovered?

OZZIE. Sure. And you?

KATE. That was the good bit of the day.

EDDIE. This is my friend, Jayne. Kate and Daniel – you know.

JAYNE. Pleased to meet you, Kate. Welcome to Zimbabwe. How are you, Daniel?

DANIEL. Good.

JAYNE. I hope you brought me some good fisheagles – the Germans can't buy enough of them.

DANIEL. I think it's more abstract stuff.

JAYNE. Then I don't need it – more than enough from Mbare at half the price.

DANIEL. So I'll get him to do fisheagles.

JAYNE. Good.

EDDIE. Jayne is the woman who buys his Uncle's sculptures – she has a gallery here.

KATE. Great.

JAYNE. I get by.

EDDIE. Who's for Chubuku?

DANIEL. I'll stick to Fanta.

KATE. Me too.

OZZIE. You got to try this stuff.

He passes the bucket to KATE.

KATE. It looks like porridge.

OZZIE. Alcoholic porridge.

EDDIE. The best kind.

JAYNE. Can't we go somewhere decent? What about the Vic Falls Hotel? I think Kate would enjoy a bit of colonial luxury. A bit better than this dump.

EDDIE. Hell no, we don't have to do that overpriced Rhodie shit.

OZZIE. It'll be full of tourists.

EDDIE. They're the worst.

JAYNE. But I want a cocktail and I'm sure your friend here isn't going to share that bucket of slop.

KATE. I'll try it.

*Chorus of approval – there is an element of competition
between* JAYNE *and* KATE. KATE *takes the bucket and
drinks from it. It is bitter but she tries to hide the distaste.*

KATE. Not bad is it?

DANIEL. You don't lie well.

EDDIE. But we appreciate the gesture.

OZZIE moves over to sit beside KATE, *the others talk in
Shona to each other.*

OZZIE. I see you've made some friends then.

KATE. Yeah. They've been great.

OZZIE. Sure – they're goodlooking guys. Which one are you
with?

KATE. Oh no, it's not like that.

OZZIE. Now I know what you meant about finding the 'real'
Africa.

KATE. I'm not going out with either of them.

OZZIE. Look, don't take this the wrong way but nice as they
seem – at some stage they'll screw you over. One way or
another. You been buying mbanje off them?

KATE. What?

OZZIE. Hash?

KATE. No.

OZZIE. You're paying them to show you around?

KATE. No. Look, you obviously have a problem understanding
that these guys are my friends. They've helped me, looked
after me, asked for nothing in return. Okay?

OZZIE. How long have you been in Africa?

KATE. A week.

OZZIE. Right.

KATE. So?

OZZIE. So I've been here three months. I've seen the Etosha Desert, the Skeleton Coast, Lake Malawi, Cape Town, Joburg. Shit I've even done Soweto. The places are fantastic but I'm telling you man, these people, these people.

KATE. Ever thought it might be you?

OZZIE. Eh?

KATE. Your attitude.

OZZIE. You're the one with the attitude. Thinking they are interested in who you are. You're a walking meal ticket.

KATE. I know who my friends are.

EDDIE. Ah, look at these whites. Always sticking to each other.

OZZIE. No mate, this one has gone native.

EDDIE. Good.

OZZIE. I'm going to catch up with some fellow travellers. Somehow I don't think we'll meet again.

He exits.

DANIEL. Problem?

KATE. No, he's a racist idiot, that's all. I'm just beginning to understand what you guys have to put up with.

EDDIE. As long as they've got the forex they can say and do as they like.

JAYNE. Now are we going somewhere decent or what? C'mon Eddie. You keep saying you know how to show a girl a good time. How about it?

EDDIE. Your wish is my command.

They get up to go.

KATE. I'll say something for Eddie.

DANIEL. What?

KATE. He is a very fast worker.

DANIEL. Jayne is an old friend.

KATE. Who he is about to get re-acquainted with.

Scene Twenty-Nine

CATHERINE *brings* JOSHUA *tea and bread. He sits up looking better.*

CATHERINE. You are almost well now.

JOSHUA *nods.*

CATHERINE. You can speak to me – I have heard you talk with Precious.

JOSHUA. I will leave soon. Tatenda.

CATHERINE. I wish you would stay. We are very happy to have you here with us.

JOSHUA. You don't know who I am or what I might have done.

ANDREW *watches them from a distance.*

CATHERINE. All I know is God brought you here.

JOSHUA. Your God.

CATHERINE. Your God too. I need your help here but I don't want you to feel you have to believe in what I believe. Just listen and learn and then make up your own mind.

JOSHUA. I will try.

She takes his hand and squeezes it, happy with his answer.

ANDREW. I see our leper has regained the power of speech.

CATHERINE. Joshua will stay with us now. He can help you I am sure.

ANDREW. My wife wants you here, but understand this – any theft or drunkenness and you are finished, do you understand me?

JOSHUA. Yes sir.

ANDREW. Let us start as we mean to go on.

CATHERINE. I don't think that was necessary.

ANDREW. Spare the rod and spoil the child, Catherine. You will learn the hard way otherwise.

Scene Thirty

DANIEL, MARTHA *and* KATE *sit on the stoop, the sounds of the night all around them.*

KATE. It's so noisy. I've never been this close to the bush before.

DANIEL. You get used to it. You are safe here in the camp. You're not frightened are you?

KATE. No. Martha, are you okay?

MARTHA *gives the thumbs up.*

DANIEL. I'm going to sleep now. We need to be up at dawn. I should be heading home and maybe the police in Bulawayo will have something.

KATE. I don't think it was a priority.

DANIEL. It's a small town – you never know. Sleep well.

KATE. Eddie's late.

DANIEL. He's always late. Remember to use your mosquito net. It's pretty bad for them up here. And don't leave the door open unless you want a warthog for company.

KATE. Okay.

DANIEL. Goodnight.

MARTHA. Goodnight.

KATE. I think you know more English than you pretend to.

MARTHA *giggles.*

KATE. Am I right?

MARTHA. Maybe. A little.

KATE. We are very close to Mozambique here, aren't we?

MARTHA *nods.*

KATE. Don't you miss your friends?

MARTHA *shakes her head.*

MARTHA. In Maputo – I sleep in the street. Men come and try to take the girls away. I come in Zimbabwe. It is good here.

KATE. And you like Eddie.

MARTHA. I love him.

KATE. You love him?

MARTHA *nods happily.*

KATE. You weren't scared on the bridge, were you?

MARTHA *giggles and* KATE *laughs too.* EDDIE *rolls in a little drunk.*

EDDIE. Ah, the Scottish woman is waiting for the Zambian drunkard. Martha, go to sleep now, eh? It's late.

MARTHA *stands up and goes. She smiles at* KATE *as she leaves.*

KATE. It's too hot to sleep yet.

EDDIE. Any better ideas?

KATE. How many women do you want in a night? Isn't Jayne enough?

EDDIE. You disappoint me Kate.

KATE. Maybe you disappoint me, Eddie.

EDDIE. Ah, ah. What have we here? You should have come for some dinner with us.

KATE. Two's company – three's a crowd.

EDDIE. I am more than man enough to handle it.

KATE. You never give up, do you. Are you ever serious?

EDDIE. Why bother? Life's too short. Take what you can get while it's going.

KATE. Is that what you were doing with Jayne?

EDDIE. Ah, c'mon, Kate – you must know by now – I'm all talk, no action. It's the best way.

KATE. So if I wanted to jump into bed with you right now, you'd turn me down.

EDDIE *is a bit taken aback by this.*

EDDIE. Eh?

KATE. That's the first time I've seen you lost for words.

EDDIE. What is this?

KATE. I'm curious, that's all.

EDDIE. I couldn't.

KATE. Fine. I thought you were teasing me. I was right.

EDDIE. No, ah – forget it – I'm drunk.

KATE. No, what were you going to say?

EDDIE. Kate, I can see it now. We kiss, then we share a bed, then – of course – you fall in love with me. We marry. Then you stay on in Zimbabwe. I go away on business, you get bored at home. You see more of Martha than me and then you get bitter, angry – you miss home, your friends there. When I come back you moan so I stay away more. I drink more. We start to fight all the time. Then you find you're pregnant and suddenly all you can think of is getting back to Scotland. So you leave. Without even telling me. You leave. And so it goes – you are a single mother in Scotland and I am a long lost father who never sees his kid.

KATE. Where was she from?

EDDIE. Canada.

KATE. And your child?

EDDIE. She's three now.

KATE. I'm sorry. I didn't realise.

EDDIE. No. That the trouble is with tourists – they want the full experience but they always want to go home in the end.

KATE. You sound so bitter.

EDDIE. Ah, it stops me getting hurt over again. It's my protection. Love them and leave them Kate. It's what I do best.

KATE. I'll get some sleep. It was nice being married to you Eddie. If only for a moment.

EDDIE. Oh Kate, did you see our children? They were so beautiful.

KATE. I'm sure they were. Goodnight.

EDDIE. Sweet dreams, sisi.

KATE. I know what I'll be dreaming of.

Scene Thirty-One

CATHERINE *and* ANDREW *are dressed for bed. Both seem awake and restless.*

CATHERINE. Never let the sun go down on your wrath.

ANDREW. I'm sorry?

CATHERINE. Never let the sun go down on your wrath. It was one of my mother's sayings. She would never let my father go to sleep until they had made up. She hated to quarrel. My father thrived on it.

ANDREW. And you?

CATHERINE. I don't like to fall out with anyone.

ANDREW. I'm not angry with you.

CATHERINE. No.

ANDREW. We have to get used to each other – that's all. There must be things which we share, which we agree on.

CATHERINE. Yes.

ANDREW. And we have to build on those things. I am not an unreasonable man.

CATHERINE. I know.

She goes to him and rubs his shoulders. Affectionately.

CATHERINE. We both want a family.

ANDREW. Definitely. That would be the making of you, I'm sure.

CATHERINE. The making of us both, perhaps.

ANDREW. Us both then.

He shakes his head, frustrated.

ANDREW. This need for correction you have.

CATHERINE. It was meant to be a compliment. I think you would make a good father – that's all.

He moves away from the physical contact, a little embarrassed.

ANDREW. I'm sorry. I'm sometimes unsure if you are making fun of me.

CATHERINE. I know I tease you at times but it is my way of showing affection.

ANDREW. And with Precious and Joshua? Do you talk about me then?

CATHERINE. No. Not in that way. This is in private between ourselves. I encourage them to look up to you. You are our minister, Andrew. We all respect what that means.

ANDREW. Good.

CATHERINE. Have I done something wrong?

ANDREW. No. I think I'll sit on the verandah for a little while.

CATHERINE. As you wish.

ANDREW. You are fortunate in having such an optimistic nature. Sometimes I feel.very burdened by what I have taken on.

CATHERINE. But your fears are groundless, Andrew.

ANDREW. Are they?

CATHERINE. Sometimes I think you worry that we'll be slaughtered in our beds.

ANDREW. It has happened.

CATHERINE. Of course. Thirty years ago missionaries were often murdered by tribal chiefs who felt threatened. My father witnessed some terrible atrocities in Matabeleland and he was fortunate to survive. Since the Boer War, all that has changed. Their sacrifice has made a pathway towards our acceptance here. We are living in a golden age.

ANDREW. You are always so clear, Catherine, so decisive.

CATHERINE. We all question ourselves at times.

ANDREW. You must think me very weak. Your father . . .

CATHERINE. My father was very driven – to the exclusion of all else. He never seemed to be able to enjoy what he had achieved. I wouldn't want you to do the same.

ANDREW. What have I achieved?

She tries to flirt with him a little to lift him out of his depression.

CATHERINE. You came here, married me. Surely you believe that to be some kind of achievement.

ANDREW. Must you turn everything I say into some kind of triviality?

CATHERINE. I didn't mean to.

ANDREW. I'm sorry. I'm sorry.

CATHERINE. We are only at the beginning.

ANDREW. As you say, this is only the start.

CATHERINE. I want you to be happy here.

ANDREW. For now.

She takes a moment before saying the next statement in a careful and measured way.

CATHERINE. I feel this talk of going back to Scotland is like a shadow hanging over us.

ANDREW. And I feel you sit in judgement on my every move.

She is exasperated with this.

CATHERINE. It'd just . . . when the rains come – we'll be able to achieve nothing if . . .

ANDREW. Catherine!

Suddenly she realises she is pushing him too much and laughs at her over-zealousness.

CATHERINE. I know. I'm sorry. Please . . . come to bed.

She looks at him and there is a moment of true tenderness and affection between them. He smiles at her.

ANDREW. Sometimes it is easier to follow, than to lead.

He goes to her. She embraces him as a mother would an uncertain child.

Scene Thirty-Two

EDDIE, MARTHA *and* DANIEL *wait outside the police station.*

EDDIE. I don't know why you made her go back to the police station. What's she going to find?

DANIEL. It's worth a try.

KATE *emerges.*

KATE. Nothing. Absolutely nothing.

EDDIE. Where next? The bank?

KATE. I can walk it.

EDDIE. Hey, we brought you this far. I can drive you another three blocks.

DANIEL. What is it, Kate?

KATE *moves away from the others and picks up a pot.*

KATE. It's the pot – the ashes. I don't believe it.

EDDIE. It can't be.

DANIEL. I knew they'd turn up.

KATE. How?

DANIEL. Juju.

EDDIE *starts laughing.*

EDDIE. You're right. I didn't think of that.

KATE. What do you mean?

DANIEL. Whoever stole them would think it was juju. And he'd be scared he'd be possessed for taking it. He's left it here so you'd find it.

KATE. You knew this would happen?

DANIEL. I knew it was possible. Sometimes superstition can be useful – even for a Christian.

KATE. I had given up hope.

EDDIE. So you going to her mission then?

KATE. Of course.

DANIEL. Good. We wish you well.

KATE. I know this is crazy but well, would you come along? All of you?

EDDIE. You need a guide – then Daniel's your man. He was born up there.

KATE. No I don't want a guide. I want your company. Please.

EDDIE. I'm up for it, bro. If you are.

DANIEL. Naw. I'll give it a miss.

EDDIE. When was the last time you saw your family up there?

DANIEL. Eddie, you know it's not easy. They're non believers. It's difficult.

EDDIE. So don't visit them. When was the last time you spent time with me, eh?

DANIEL. We can do that anytime.

EDDIE. Except we don't. Look, she won't go with me alone.

KATE. I understand. You have your parish to get back to. Your family.

DANIEL. Well, my parish will still be standing when I get back.

EDDIE. Good. Why am I saying good? It's going to kill my Benz – you realise that.

KATE. And Martha can come?

EDDIE. Only if she travels on the roof rack.

KATE *and* DANIEL. Eddie!

EDDIE. Joke! It was a joke.

MARTHA *gives the thumbs up.*

EDDIE. Why am I helping you people. I must be out of my mind.

Scene Thirty-Three

PRECIOUS *and* CATHERINE *are working together.*

CATHERINE. I heard there was trouble in the village.

PRECIOUS. Yes. They say it was a young girl. She gave birth. It was twins. They were going to kill the babies but she ran away into the bush.

CATHERINE. Why do they believe twins to be a curse?

PRECIOUS. I don't know. It is bad spirits who do this. They lie with a woman. The mother is cursed. It makes me feel afraid to have a baby.

CATHERINE. I think it would be better for you to have a husband first.

PRECIOUS. Yes.

CATHERINE. If you were baptised you would have nothing to fear.

PRECIOUS. If this girl came here – you would take her in.

CATHERINE. Of course. She is here, already isn't she?

A YOUNG GIRL *emerges from the shadows. She kneels before* CATHERINE. CATHERINE *kneels down beside her and takes her in her arms. The* GIRL *weeps.* CATHERINE *looks at* PRECIOUS.

CATHERINE. Where are the babies?

PRECIOUS. We have hidden them. They are safe.

CATHERINE. Good. Make her comfortable and feed her. She will need her strength.

PRECIOUS. She can stay?

CATHERINE. Yes. But you must make her understand that she cannot leave the compound. The Chief will be very angry. He will want those babies killed.

PRECIOUS. What will the master say?

CATHERINE. He knows little of these atrocities. It is better that I tell him later. I know he is keen to win favour with the Chief. He feels his conversion will secure our future here.

PRECIOUS. Will God make everything good?

CATHERINE. I wish I could say that, Precious but I can't. Bad things still happen. We both know that. My father died. But that is the will of God, you have to accept it.

Scene Thirty-Four

MARTHA, DANIEL, EDDIE *and* KATE *travel along together.* MARTHA *sings to herself.*

KATE. So what would you be doing if you weren't here now?

DANIEL. Visiting the sick. Working out my sermon for Sunday.

EDDIE. This should give you plenty new material. A few days in hell with Eddie, the lost soul. And you, Kate?

KATE. Probably watching the telly. Maybe seeing friends.

DANIEL. Fanta?

KATE. Please.

DANIEL *gives* KATE *a Fanta from the coolbox and takes one for himself but doesn't offer* EDDIE *one. Without taking his eyes off the road,* EDDIE *is aware of this.*

EDDIE. No, not for me. Thank you – I'm fine. Just fine.

KATE *and* DANIEL *exchange a smile.*

DANIEL (*Shona*). Pani chauri kuda? (Would you like something?)

EDDIE (*Shona*). Aiwa. Mutyairi aribho. Maita henyu. (No, the chauffeur is doing fine. Thank you.)

KATE. If it wasn't so dry, it'd be like the Scottish Highlands.

DANIEL. People get lost in the mountains.

KATE. In Scotland too.

EDDIE. Hey, minister – you Christians aren't allowed to believe in such things. It's for us heathens to believe there are spirits in there.

KATE. You go hillwalking?

EDDIE. No way. Walkers disappear and then come back, years later – but not a day older. Spooky eh? How does your God explain that?

DANIEL. I didn't realise he was on trial.

EDDIE. It is what God put heathens on earth for. And you Kate? You a believer?

KATE. I don't know.

EDDIE. You don't know!

DANIEL. But your gran was . . .

KATE. Yes, my gran. I wish I had her faith. Simple. Trusting. I feel like a tired old cynic, reluctant to commit to anything.

EDDIE. I like that. Your ancestors came here to teach us what to believe. Now you've come here to tell us not to bother in all that any more. You got it wrong. Now that I can believe.

KATE. Eddie, that's not what I'm saying.

DANIEL. Or have you come here to find God?

EDDIE. If we're getting a sermon, you can walk.

KATE. I don't know.

DANIEL. It's very common. People from the West, getting close to nature and themselves finding some spirituality. It's not real though.

KATE. No?

DANIEL. It's part of their holiday. An escape. When they get back to work, they are too busy to wonder what they're doing it all for. What life is about.

EDDIE. For once, you're right. Sometimes I'm sitting watching a sunset with a cold beer in one hand and a Pentax in another. There you can think – wow, amazing – there must be a God to create something as beautiful as this. Then the moment's gone, the beer is finished, you move on.

KATE. I didn't come to Africa to find God. If I was into all that, I'd have gone to India or Tibet.

DANIEL. I didn't know God only existed in certain countries.

EDDIE. Why am I here? Why did I agree to do this? If there is a God, please take Daniel from this car or get him to shut up. Now that would be a miracle.

DANIEL. Am I boring you?

KATE. We haven't mentioned women, money or sex for at least ten minutes. Of course we're boring Eddie.

EDDIE. And this from the woman who claims she can't take care of herself.

KATE. It's a long way.

DANIEL. It is in this car.

EDDIE. The sky is getting dark. The rains are coming. We'll need to stop overnight in the village.

KATE. Is that okay?

DANIEL. We've come this far now. There's no point turning back.

KATE. If you're sure.

DANIEL. I'm sure.

EDDIE. Come on baby, let's get to Nyanga village before the sun goes down.

Scene Thirty-Five

JOSHUA *is up high working away on the roof.* PRECIOUS *is below beating grain with a wooden pole. She sings an African song in time with her action.*

CATHERINE *comes out looking very happy. She calls up to* JOSHUA.

CATHERINE. Come down, I've made tea.

PRECIOUS. That is for me to do.

CATHERINE. Let me feel useful, will you? You have both worked so hard.

JOSHUA takes his tea. He smiles at PRECIOUS.

JOSHUA. Thank you.

CATHERINE. No, thank you. We have a chance now of finishing the roof before the rains. Then I hope the first baptism will be yours, Precious.

PRECIOUS. We shall see.

CATHERINE. We are your family now. What would your Christian name be? What would you like?

PRECIOUS. The minister always chooses.

CATHERINE. I know but I do have a little influence there. And you, Joshua? We've already baptised you informally. Won't you accept Christ in your life?

He shrugs non-committally.

CATHERINE. It's not something I want to push you into. You will know in your heart what is right for you.

PRECIOUS. When did you know?

CATHERINE. Oh, I'm not sure. I've always known I suppose. I grew up believing – it would be strange for me not to.

PRECIOUS. We have our ancestral spirits – that is what we grow up with. They live with us, guiding us. That is what we believe.

CATHERINE. And you too, Joshua?

JOSHUA. Of course. It is our tradition. But you don't have that?

CATHERINE. Well, we believe in heaven and hell so your spirit exists after death but where it ends up depends on how you have lived your life. If you have lived a good life, helping others – then you have nothing to fear but if you have sinned, gone against God by breaking his commandments – like killing someone – then you will be damned.

PRECIOUS. Has God brought us here? To you?

CATHERINE. I believe he has. When Jesus came to earth, he walked with the poor, the outcasts and even the prostitutes. Now look as us – each of us cast out in our own way, isolated and alone, yet together we make a family.

PRECIOUS. But you chose this life – we did not.

CATHERINE. No. I believe that God chose this life for me and so I accept it.

ANDREW *comes in looking a little wary of their closeness.*

ANDREW. May I join you?

CATHERINE. You have arrived at the right moment. We were having a discussion about heaven and hell.

ANDREW. Is this you preaching now?

CATHERINE. No, we were discussing spirits.

JOSHUA *and* PRECIOUS *look a little uncomfortable at* ANDREW's *presence.* JOSHUA *gets to his feet and climbs the ladder once more.*

CATHERINE. Joshua!

PRECIOUS. He must work, ma'am. I will get the master a cup of tea.

ANDREW. Why are they so scared of me?

CATHERINE. It's not you. It is because you are the minister. I think they are scared of committing themselves to Christianity. It will cut them off from their own people.

ANDREW. Not for long – soon others will follow. If we are courageous enough to come to this continent, then surely they can be brave enough to embrace what we have to give them.

CATHERINE. You're right. It takes courage.

ANDREW. But they trust you.

CATHERINE. A little.

ANDREW. So you must try harder.

CATHERINE. They work for us – that is why they are here. I don't want to push them away by forcing them to convert.

ANDREW. If we can't convert them, what hope do we have?

Scene Thirty-Six

KATE *is sitting outside and* EDDIE *joins her.*

EDDIE. Hey Kate. It's not the Sheraton eh?

KATE. My room is fine.

EDDIE. Mine isn't. No minibar! I am used to five star treatment. I'm going to the bottle store. Can your legs make it?

KATE. I'll stay here, if that's okay.

EDDIE. Sure. I'll bring you back a couple, yeah?

KATE. I think Martha wants to come with you.

EDDIE. Great.

KATE. Yeah.

EDDIE *walks off followed happily by* MARTHA. DANIEL *emerges when* EDDIE *has gone.*

KATE. Eddie is off to the bottle store. If you hurry, you'll catch him.

DANIEL. And if I sit down, I won't.

He sits down.

KATE. Okay?

DANIEL. Sure. They're cooking us some sadza, my bed is comfortable. What more could I want?

KATE. To be at home with your family. You've put yourself out for me. I feel bad about that.

DANIEL. Don't. Maybe this is my holiday too.

KATE. You don't get away much?

DANIEL. Us Zimbabweans – we work in town in the week then at weekends and at holiday time go back to our rural home. There is always a lot to do.

KATE. But you're happy.

DANIEL. Your words not mine. I get by. Apartheid leaves its legacy you know? Things don't come right just because people get the right to vote.

KATE. But it's such a fundamental right.

DANIEL. So is free education and healthcare but those have gone. The people I see need that, more than they need me most of the time.

KATE. It's happening to us in the U.K. too.

DANIEL. Don't let that happen, Kate. People need basic human rights – to allow them to live and die with dignity. Sometimes religion is simply not enough.

KATE. Are you allowed to say that?

DANIEL. I'm on my holidays. I can say what I like.

KATE. I thought having faith made things easier.

DANIEL. Not necessarily. I am not the kind of person who can tell people who are suffering that it's okay – they will have their reward in the next life. Telling people that only allows injustice to thrive.

KATE. I see what you mean. Maybe one day when economically things are better – maybe then it will be better for your country. Like it is for us in Scotland.

DANIEL. I don't want us to be like you.

KATE. No?

DANIEL. Has it ever occurred to you that we might have got it right? That what is ruining our country and our culture now is Capitalism and the push to be like the West?

KATE. We're not forcing that on you. It's your government's choice.

DANIEL. I think people have very little choice. Rural farmers don't grow food to feed their families any more, they grow tobacco – a cash crop. It makes the farmer dependent on trade and somehow, it's always these people who lose out.

KATE. Is that why you're so bitter?

DANIEL. I'm bitter because people come to me for answers. Why did my sister die? Why do my crops fail? And all the time, I try to give them answers, I offer them comfort. I sit with them, pray with them and pretend I understand.

KATE. Well, that's good. You try your best.

DANIEL. Then my own wife loses our first born and suddenly all words seem empty and nothing can bring me comfort. I am the minister, yet I am so angry with God for taking away our joy, I cannot help myself or anyone else.

KATE. You have helped me.

DANIEL. Anyone could have helped you.

KATE. That's not true. I wanted to give up, turn back and that would have made me feel like such a failure. I have a lot to thank you for.

DANIEL. I was so angry that day on the train. I wanted to run away from everything. Going to the Falls for my Uncle was a good excuse to leave it all behind.

KATE. But you feel a little better now?

DANIEL. Being with Eddie makes me remember what it was like when I was younger. We were very stupid boys but we had some great times together.

EDDIE *arrives with* MARTHA *following.*

EDDIE. Hey guys – We bought the bottle store!

KATE. And Martha got to carry them all. What a surprise.

Scene Thirty-Seven

JOSHUA *sits whittling away on a mbezo (piece of wood).*
CATHERINE *comes and joins him. He stands up and she*
indicates for him to sit. She pulls up a little African stool and
sits down. She watches him work.

CATHERINE. I wish I could carve.

JOSHUA *offers her the mbezo and the knife.*

CATHERINE. No, I couldn't.

JOSHUA *still holds it out, refusing to take no for an answer.*

She takes the stick and the knife and chips away nervously
taking out a tiny sliver. He takes the knife back and shows
her how to cut by example. The next time she tries, it is
more confident and she is pleased with herself.

CATHERINE. Ah, that's better. You're a good teacher, Joshua.
When we finally get a school open, maybe you could help
the boys learn some practical skills.

JOSHUA *shrugs non-committally.*

CATHERINE. Do you understand much English?

JOSHUA *nods.*

CATHERINE. This juju that you wear. I have been wanting to
talk to you about it – you don't mind, do you?

JOSHUA *shakes his head.*

CATHERINE. It's a problem for me. My husband feels it is
bad if someone working here and living here is wearing
something so much connected – well, with witchcraft. It is
as though we condone it and you know, Joshua, that we
don't. It is wrong and can be very very harmful. I know you
feel it protects you but . . . that is what Christ does surely.
We are here to look after each other, Joshua. You don't need
anything to ward off evil spirits anymore.

JOSHUA (*Shona*). My name is Munyaradzi.

CATHERINE. But we all know you as . . .

JOSHUA (*Shona*). My name is Munyaradzi.

CATHERINE. I have offended you. I am sorry.

JOSHUA. I was someone before I came here. I had a life.

CATHERINE. I understand you and I am sorry.

JOSHUA. No, you have been kind to me and to Precious. She is very fond of you.

CATHERINE. And I of her.

JOSHUA. I want to marry Precious. But she will only marry as a Christian now. She believes in you.

CATHERINE. But that is wonderful.

JOSHUA. I do not know what I want. But I want her for my wife. If I have to become a Christian, then perhaps it will be worth it for her.

CATHERINE. But you must do it for yourself also. But giving up your Juju isn't like converting – it is only a step in that direction.

He is silent. CATHERINE *gets to her feet and starts to walk away. She turns back to look at him.*

He takes the knife and cuts the leather cord from around his throat and holds it out to her.

CATHERINE. God bless you.

Scene Thirty-Eight

EDDIE, KATE, DANIEL *and* MARTHA.

EDDIE. They say there is no working mission here.

KATE. Well, that's rubbish. Gran showed me the place on the map.

MARTHA. Fanta?

DANIEL. Not now. Martha.

EDDIE. There's someone that might help us.

KATE. Who?

EDDIE. The nyanga.

KATE. There's one here?

EDDIE. She's only a tourist attraction but it's worth a try.

DANIEL. No. Don't even think about it.

KATE. Why not?

DANIEL. You shouldn't play with these things. Don't you understand that?

KATE. I'm sorry but I've come this far.

EDDIE. Daniel, let her go. Your family brought you up with it all and you've rejected it but Kate has to find out for herself.

DANIEL. Find out what? How to steal someone's footprint and fry it with salt so you can put a spell on them.

KATE. What?

DANIEL. Maybe get some juju to use on your ex-boyfriend to get your revenge.

KATE. I wouldn't do that.

EDDIE. She needs some answers – that's all.

DANIEL. I'll come with you then. I'd like some answers too.

Scene Thirty-Nine

CATHERINE *dangles the little juju bag before* ANDREW's *face. He is deeply immersed in his writing and looks mildly irritated at being disturbed.*

CATHERINE. For you.

ANDREW. What is it?

CATHERINE. Juju.

ANDREW. I don't understand.

CATHERINE. A little bag of special herbs to ward off evil spirits. People wear it for protection.

ANDREW. Against witchcraft.

CATHERINE. Yes.

ANDREW. And where did you find it?

CATHERINE. Joshua gave it to me.

ANDREW. Why?

CATHERINE. I think it's his first step towards us. He wants to marry Precious and she has told him she could only have a Christian marriage.

ANDREW. And you believe him.

CATHERINE. Why would he lie?

ANDREW. To impress you.

CATHERINE. It means a lot Andrew – please, trust in him as I do. If we don't have faith, what's left?

ANDREW. I know you want to believe the best in these people but remember, they are without education, moral guidance. It is up to Joshua to put his faith in us not the other way around.

CATHERINE. He will.

ANDREW. I thought there were more influential converts which we could persuade.

CATHERINE. I'm sure there are.

ANDREW. The chief himself wished to meet with me.

CATHERINE. Why, that's wonderful news.

ANDREW. Till he found we were harbouring a possessed girl and her children. Now he will have nothing to do with us. What are you trying to do, Catherine. Put our lives in danger?

CATHERINE. He would have killed her. I had no choice.

ANDREW. Who are you to decide these things?

CATHERINE. I am your wife. What if I were to have twins, Andrew? Would you protect me?

ANDREW. That is a completely different matter. If that were to happen then . . .

CATHERINE. It could. I am carrying your child.

ANDREW. That is wonderful news.

CATHERINE. I hoped you would be happy, Andrew. Now you must see, I could not turn a young mother away. My heart went out to her.

ANDREW. You let your heart rule your head.

CATHERINE. It is the only way I know.

ANDREW. All I want for us is to be happy.

CATHERINE. I will try to make that happen, Andrew. Believe me.

Scene Forty

KATE *kneels in front of a woman who sits on the floor.* EDDIE *and* DANIEL *stand behind her.* DANIEL *looks very uncomfortable.*

EDDIE. Masikati Ambuya.

NYANGA. I speak English. I speak to the woman only. You men must go.

KATE. I'll be alright. It is good of you to see me.

NYANGA. You are sad.

KATE. Yes.

NYANGA. Someone you love has passed.

KATE. Yes. They were born here. This was her homeland. She was happy here.

NYANGA. No. She brought sorrow.

KATE. No, you don't understand. She worked here – she was a missionary.

NYANGA. You must go to the place of tears.

KATE. No, that isn't the place. She built a mission. A church.

NYANGA. That is the place I cannot tell you more. What do you want from me? Some juju?

KATE. No, all I want is to find that place – see where she lived.

NYANGA. I have nice thing to help you get a baby.

KATE. I don't need that. I don't even have a boyfriend.

NYANGA. A potion to give you a man. You put it on his food and he will never look at another woman.

KATE. No. I'm sorry I came. This is wrong. My gran would have hated this.

NYANGA. There is nothing for you here. You must go now. Other people are waiting.

KATE. How much?

NYANGA. Ten dollar.U.S.

Scene Forty-One

PRECIOUS *is using a reed brush to sweep away the dust from the floor. She is bent low as* ANDREW *sits at his desk reading. He looks up and watches at her effort.*

ANDREW. You are a very hard worker, Do you know that?

PRECIOUS. Thank you, Sir. I try.

ANDREW. Will you sit down for a moment, please.

PRECIOUS *sits down but does not look comfortable with this situation.*

ANDREW. I hear that you are thinking about getting married.

PRECIOUS. No, sir.

ANDREW. No?

She shakes her head.

ANDREW. Joshua told my wife . . .

PRECIOUS. We have talked about marriage. It is true.

ANDREW. And?

PRECIOUS. And when I know him better, then I can decide.

ANDREW. Very wise. You have an old head on young shoulders. Well, I should be delighted to marry you, should you decide he is the right man. Of course, you would both have to be baptised into the faith before you could have a Christian marriage – you know that.

PRECIOUS. Yes. Can I go now?

ANDREW. Certainly – I don't want to keep you from your chores. Precious?

She turns.

ANDREW. You are not afraid that Joshua might leave, go back to his own people?

PRECIOUS. No. He is very happy here. Your wife is very kind to him, to all of us.

ANDREW. Yes, she is very popular.

Scene Forty-Two

They are in the car together. All are quiet.

KATE. She said the place of tears.

EDDIE. You know it?

DANIEL. Yes. I was hoping it wasn't there – that there had been a mission I didn't know about.

KATE. You knew about this place all along.

DANIEL. Yes. It is only some ruins. It has been empty for years.

KATE. Then why put me through that?

DANIEL. That was what you wanted? Remember – the juju and the witchdoctor. You told me that what you believed in.

KATE. All she believes in is the US dollar. I could visit Gypsy Rose Lee in Glasgow and get as much for a fiver.

EDDIE. She's not a real one. Just a cheap fake.

DANIEL. You still want to go there?

KATE. Of course. I know it's not the fairytale she told me but it still the place she wanted to end her days. Whatever happened there.

Scene Forty-Three

CATHERINE *is making the bed.* PRECIOUS *comes and joins her.*

PRECIOUS. Can I help you?

CATHERINE. Please.

They make up the bed together standing at opposite sides. They are easy and relaxed with each other.

CATHERINE. Soon you will be making a bed for you and Joshua.

PRECIOUS. Maybe.

CATHERINE. Don't be shy. I see you are in love with him.

PRECIOUS. How?

CATHERINE. The way you look at him.

CATHERINE *indicates for* PRECIOUS *to sit with her on the edge of the bed. She does so.*

CATHERINE. Don't think I don't notice because I do.

CATHERINE *is being playful and fun but* PRECIOUS *looks more serious.*

PRECIOUS. Do you miss your father?

CATHERINE. Yes, of course. Why do you ask me that?

PRECIOUS. He was a very good man.

CATHERINE. And Andrew isn't?

PRECIOUS. I am sure he is.

CATHERINE. You don't like him, Do you? Be honest with me.

PRECIOUS. I am afraid for you.

CATHERINE. Why?

PRECIOUS. Because you are stronger than him.

CATHERINE. Not at all.

PRECIOUS. And he is jealous of that.

CATHERINE. Precious – what put this idea into your head?

PRECIOUS. No. I'm sorry. I am being foolish.

CATHERINE. Please – what is all this about?

PRECIOUS. I must go now.

CATHERINE. Andrew is insecure – that's all. Africa – the mission – it's all still very new to him. Believe in him, Precious, as I must.

PRECIOUS *only nods and goes out, leaving* CATHERINE *looking pensive.*

Scene Forty-Four

DANIEL, EDDIE, MARTHA *and* KATE *walk onto the ground. They gaze around, looking a little bewildered.*

KATE. It's so desolate.

EDDIE. Nothing but stones eh? Great view. You could build a nice house for weekends up here.

DANIEL. It's too far to drive.

EDDIE. Yeah. They were keen those missionaries.

KATE. It's true what they say. It is better to travel hopefully than it is to arrive.

EDDIE. Not quite what you were expecting.

KATE. No.

EDDIE. Sorry about that.

KATE. Don't be. You brought me here and I'm grateful. I'd have been kicking myself if I'd not seen it for myself.

DANIEL. It has always been deserted. No one wanted to build here.

KATE. Why?

DANIEL. A Shona legend. Some man went missing in the mountains and his sweetheart grew old waiting for him to come back.

EDDIE. Wouldn't be me. I'd have waited half an hour – then hey, life goes on.

DANIEL. What a romantic.

EDDIE. Yeah! Shall I get the ghetto blaster from the car? And the coolbox – we could have a picnic?

DANIEL *and* KATE: No.!

EDDIE. Okay, okay. I'll see you guys back in the car. Yeah?

KATE. No stay. I'm going to bury the ashes. Maybe we could – I don't know – say a prayer or something.

EDDIE. You'll need to be quick. There's a storm brewing.

KATE. It won't take long.

Scene Forty-Five

PRECIOUS *is gathering things to take inside. The sky is dark.* JOSHUA *is helping her.* CATHERINE *comes out and joins in.*

CATHERINE. It's going to be quite a storm.

PRECIOUS. I need to get the cattle into the kraal.

CATHERINE. Yes. Hurry. Munyaradzi, let me help.

They carry bundles of wood inside.

What would we do without you?

JOSHUA *only shrugs.*

CATHERINE. I hope you and Precious will marry and stay with us. It would make me very happy.

She touches his arm and he smiles. ANDREW *appears in the doorway. He looks at this gesture of affection with disdain.* JOSHUA *gets to his feet and goes outside.* ANDREW *stands watching* CATHERINE *and when he speaks it is cold and without emotion.*

ANDREW. Someone has been killed in the village.

CATHERINE. How?

ANDREW. By a lion. It must be injured or old. The beast is very dangerous now. We should get the cattle into the kraal and stay inside.

CATHERINE. Precious is already doing that. The villagers will go out as a group and destroy it.

ANDREW. I must go after it.

CATHERINE. No.

ANDREW. But I must.

CATHERINE. The sky is darkening. The rains are coming.

ANDREW. Don't you see it's my chance now.

CATHERINE. You've never seen one of the storms – it would be madness.

ANDREW. I know what I'm doing.

CATHERINE. Andrew, I beg you . . .

ANDREW. Don't you see? This is a sign? This is God giving me the opportunity to prove to these people that we have been sent here with a purpose. I am not afraid. I feel protected.

CATHERINE. But when the rains come?

ANDREW. We will shelter.

CATHERINE. Who is going with you?

ANDREW. I am going to take Joshua. I need a guide. And you trust him, don't you? He is your friend.

CATHERINE. He will not want to go.

ANDREW. He is my employee. He will come.

JOSHUA *appears in the doorway.*

ANDREW. Come with me. I need you to track for me. This lion must be killed without delay.

JOSHUA (*Shona*). Handifungi kuti mfundisi vano fanira kudaro. (Ma'am. The preacher is unwise.)

ANDREW. Don't talk to her – talk to me.

CATHERINE (*Shona*). Andisikuda kuti kuende munhu ikoko (I do not want either of you to go.)

ANDREW. I told you, Catherine. I forbid you to speak in that heathen language ever again.

CATHERINE. Please Andrew. Believe me, you should not go. Either of you. I fear for your lives.

ANDREW *picks up his gun and looks at* JOSHUA.

ANDREW. I have a duty, to myself and my God. I believe we have to go and kill this lion. Then I will be respected, then they will show me the respect they showed your father. Come, Joshua – we must go.

JOSHUA *does not move.*

ANDREW. You see? This is what I am talking about. He will not move for me. Tell him to come with me.

CATHERINE. I cannot ask him to . . .

ANDREW. You cannot or will not. I am your husband and you will obey me. Tell him to come with me.

CATHERINE. I do not want to ask this of you but I must. You know that. Please Munyaradzi, go with my husband and make sure that both of you are safe.

He goes with ANDREW. *They leave together without looking back.* CATHERINE *sits down, looking shattered.* PRECIOUS *stands alone.*

It is dark. CATHERINE *calls out to her.*

CATHERINE. You must sleep now.

PRECIOUS *shakes her head.* CATHERINE *comes and leads her gently towards her bed.*

CATHERINE. We must have faith. Sleep now. Joy cometh in the morning.

Scene Forty-Six

*The spirits return. The mbira is played, then the drumming
comes in. The demons appear with their masks and their
rattles and their frenetic and inisistent motion. They become
louder and faster and the sound of the rain falling can be
heard. Torrential rain beating down. Then all is still. The
demons disappear and the watery light of early morning.*

Scene Forty-Seven

The dawn comes and ANDREW *stands alone without his gun.*
CATHERINE *stands some distance apart.*

CATHERINE. Where is Munyaradzi?

ANDREW. I lost him in the hills.

CATHERINE. And your gun?

ANDREW. Lost too.

CATHERINE. You didn't find the lion.

ANDREW. No. I need to sleep now.

CATHERINE. What happened, Andrew?

ANDREW. I don't remember. I'm very tired now.

CATHERINE. Andrew.

> ANDREW *looks as though he is on the verge of collapse.
> She goes and holds him in her arms to support him but
> without affection. He looks at her and touches her stomach.*

ANDREW. This will be my son.

CATHERINE. Or daughter.

> ANDREW *breaks down weeping.*

ANDREW. I'm so sorry, Catherine. I'm so sorry.

CATHERINE. We need to go back to Scotland.

ANDREW. I have tried so hard.

CATHERINE. I will start packing right away. You must go home now.

ANDREW. And you will come with me?

CATHERINE. What choice do I have?

ANDREW. Catherine – you have asked me nothing.

CATHERINE. Let God be your judge, not me.

ANDREW *lies down, exhausted.*

CATHERINE *goes to* PRECIOUS.

PRECIOUS. Where is Joshua?

CATHERINE. He . . . they went into the mountains together. They were separated. Andrew came back alone.

PRECIOUS. How could he come back without him?

CATHERINE. I don't know.

PRECIOUS. We trusted in you – both of us.

CATHERINE. I know. You must have faith now, Precious – pray for his safe return.

PRECIOUS. He is to be my husband. He must come back. He is strong. He knows the way and God . . . God will help him.

CATHERINE. If he can. Andrew – he – it was a mistake for him to come here. He doesn't have the strength. He is a weak man, you know that, don't you?

PRECIOUS *nods.*

PRECIOUS. You will have to take him back to Scotland.

CATHERINE. Yes.

PRECIOUS. You are going to leave me?

CATHERINE. I have no choice. If I could take you with us, then I would but you know that I can't.

PRECIOUS. No. I will wait for my Munyaradzi. My Joshua. I will have faith. Read to me while I wait.

CATHERINE *reads from the Bible. Her words are heartfelt.*

CATHERINE.
Why standest thou afar off, O Lord?
Why hidest thou thyself in times of trouble?
The wicked in his pride doth persecute the poor:
let them be taken in the devices they have imagined.
For the wicked boasteth of his heart's desire,
And blesseth the covetous whom the Lord abhorreth.
The wicked, through the pride of his countenance will
    not seek after God:
God is not in all his thoughts . . .
Lord, thou hast heard the desire of the humble:
thou wilt prepare their heart, thou wilt cause thine ear
    to hear:
To judge the fatherless and the oppressed,
that the man of the earth may no more oppress.

CATHERINE. I wanted us to be happy here. To be a family.

PRECIOUS. Yes.

CATHERINE. I am pregnant. I am having his child.

CATHERINE *weeps and* PRECIOUS *weeps with her. They embrace.*

Scene Forty-Eight

KATE *has finished putting the ashes in the ground. She stands up and looks at others.* DANIEL, MARTHA *and* EDDIE *stand together.*

KATE. I'm a bit embarrassed dragging you all up here.

DANIEL. Don't be.

KATE. I thought it would be thriving. She talked so lovingly about it. It was all there. In her mind.

DANIEL. What happened to your grandfather?

KATE. He died hillwalking in the Scotland – the weather closed in on them. He was only forty-two. Gran brought my mum and her brothers up alone. She managed. My parents moved up to Skye when I was fifteen and I stayed on with Gran. Didn't want to leave my school or my pals.

DANIEL. She must have liked that.

KATE. Most of the time – I was a bit of a handful then. So this was her youth – here. There is nothing to show that she was here.

EDDIE. You came here. That means something.

KATE. Could you, Daniel – say a few words?

DANIEL. I thought I was on my holidays.

KATE. It would mean a lot to me.

DANIEL. I don't know if I can.

EDDIE. Help me out here, bro. It's either you or me and it's not going to sound very good coming from an atheist.

MARTHA *sings 'Amazing Grace' in Shona.*

DANIEL. For I am the Way, the Truth and the Life. Teach me what to believe, what to do and wherein to find thy peace. for thine own name sake we ask it. Amen.

KATE. Thank you, Daniel. I wish I could make a cross or something.

DANIEL. Leave something. Make your mark.

KATE. I don't have anything . . .

EDDIE. Hold on.

EDDIE *disappears and comes back with the little stone sculpture wrapped in the towel.*

KATE. I couldn't.

EDDIE. Daniel is taking it back to his Uncle. It didn't sell.

DANIEL. I'd like you to have it.

MARTHA. Please.

EDDIE. We'll wait for you in the car. Come on, Martha. I'll get you a Fanta.

They leave.

She gives it to him and accepts the sculpture.

DANIEL. For you.

They exchange a Shona handshake.

She puts the sculpture down on the ground. She does not look at him as she speaks.

KATE. Are you alright?

DANIEL. I need to go home now. I'm ready.

KATE. Good. I wouldn't have made it here without you.

DANIEL. I think you know how to take care of yourself.

KATE. No, you're the one who took care of me.

DANIEL. Well, maybe we were meant to meet. I believe everything happens for a reason.

KATE. Now you're talking like a minister again.

DANIEL. Perhaps. And where for you now? Home to Scotland?

KATE. No. I'm going to keep travelling. Zanzibar. I fancy that.

DANIEL. I'm sure Eddie could sort out a flight.

KATE. I think I need to move on alone, don't you?

DANIEL. Maybe. I'll leave you to say goodbye.

KATE *looks at the stone. She touches the red earth around it. She pours a little liquid on the ground and smiles.*

She exits leaving the stone sitting alone on the stage.

The end.

A Nick Hern Book

The Juju Girl first published in Great Britain in 1999
as an original paperback by Nick Hern Books Limited,
14 Larden Road, London W3 7ST, in association with
the Traverse Theatre, Edinburgh

The Juju Girl copyright © Aileen Ritchie 1999

Aileen Ritchie has asserted her right to be identified as
author of this work

Typeset by Country Setting, Kingsdown, Kent CT14 8ES

Printed and bound in Great Britain by Cox & Wyman Ltd,
Reading, Berks

A CIP catalogue record for this book is available from the
British Library

ISBN 1-85459-462-1

CAUTION   All rights whatsoever in this play are strictly
reserved. Requests to reproduce the text in whole or in part
should be addressed to Nick Hern Books.

Amateur Performing Rights   Applications for performance
in excerpt or in full by non-professionals in English throughout
the world (excluding USA and Canada) should be addressed to
Nick Hern Books Limited 14 Larden Road, London W3 7ST,
fax + 44 (0) 208-746-2006, *e-mail* info@nickhernbooks.demon.co.uk

Professional Performing Rights   Applications for performance
by professionals (and for amateur and stock performance rights
in USA and Canada) in any medium and in any language
throughout the world should be addressed to Casarotto Ramsay
and Associates, National House, 60-66 Wardour Street, London
W1V 3HP

No performance of any kind may be given unless a licence has
been obtained. Application should be made before rehearsals
begin.